pompom

minipom

HAPPY KNITS FOR LITTLE KIDS

Mini Pom
Published in 2022 by Pom Pom Press
Text and Illustrations © 2022 Pom Pom Press
Photography © 2022 Laura Morsman

ISBN: 978-1-7391075-0-5

A catalogue record for this book is available from the British Library.

Pattern Design + Writing: Meghan Fernandes (Mini Skipworth, Mini Pom Scarf, Mini Lobelia), Lydia Gluck (Mini Woodwardia, Mini Norn), Sophie Heathscott (Truffle), Rachel Coopey (Mini Shirley), Fiona Alice (Mini Take Heart), Kiyomi Burgin + Sachiko Burgin (Mini Kordy), Gina Fama Röckenwagner (Mini Battenberg), Toshiyuki Shimada (Pinwheel Blanket)

Additional Pattern Writing: Alice Sleight, Chaitanya Muralidhara + Laura Chau

Editors + Creative Directors: Lydia Gluck + Meghan Fernandes

Managing Editor: Amy Collins

Design + Layout: Bless

Pattern Photography: Laura Morsman

Tutorial Writing: Sophie Heathscott

Publisher + Marketing Director: Belinda Johnson

UK Wholesale Manager + Community Liaison: Sophie Heathscott

US Wholesale Manager: Jasmine Payne

Features Editor: Francesca Baldry

Production Coordinator + Retail Manager: Alice Sleight

Social Media + Digital Content Coordinator: Sofia Aatkar

Studio Managers: Anoushka Hartounian + Gayle Taliaferro Gilner

Technical Editors: Chaitanya Muralidhara, Laura Chau + Jemima Bicknell

Pattern + Tutorial Illustrations: Lydia Gluck

Copy Editor: Annie Prime

Consultant: Emi Ito

Models: Avienne, Camila, Loden, Lola, Royce, Sabine, Sylvie

Location: The Cute House, Austin, Texas

Yarn Support: BC Garn, Berroco, Hedgehog Fibres, John Arbon Textiles, Kelbourne Woolens, Malabrigo, Manos del Uruguay, Neighborhood Fiber Co., Purl Soho, Qing Fibre, Rauma Garn, Retrosaria Rosa Pomar, The Uncommon Thread, The Wandering Flock

Sample knitters: Chaitanya Muralidhara, Chonita Olivas, Kelly Jensen Sembos, Meghan Fernandes, Rebecca Yohe, Sophie Heathscott

Test Knitters: Alexandra Shcherbakova, Amber Burton, Anne-Marie Fairhurst, Anoush Emrazian Anderson, Beate Nolte, Bettina, Cardner Babakitis, Cassie Lange, Chantal Reininger, Christin Tapsell, Christine Dildine, Diana Pellegrino, Emily Dupras-Carcélès, Emily Tindall, Erin Warlow, Eva Jonsson, Gayle Gansch, Heather Ellis, Jacqui Zurawski, Jane M Hosking, Janet Chang, Kate Lindstrom, Katt Weaver, Kellen Chang Boucher, Kristin Irgens, Kristina Russell, Lauren Cyders, Lauryl Fine, Liz Tyson, Maria Dooley, Mariana Tuma, Marie-Christine Boeve, Maya McNichol, Melissa Thompson, Min-young Han, Nicola Nicholson, Nicola Sheehan, Orlane Bienfait-Luna, Patrice Safarik, Petra Kime, Rachel Erne, Samantha Geary, Sara Rabideau, Sarah Fisher, Sarah Friend, Sheri Newberger, Sophie Heathscott, Stacey Rivera, Suzanne Stallard, Terri Cook, Veena Mosur, Veronica Jackson, Virpi Sipelaeinen

For pattern corrections, please visit: *pompommag.com/errata*

Printed sustainably in the UK by Pureprint Group Limited, a CarbonNeutral® Company with FSC® chain of custody and an ISO 14001 certified environmental management system recycling over 99% of all dry waste. The paper is Carbon Balanced with the World Land Trust™, an international conservation charity, who offset carbon emissions through the purchase and preservation of high conservation value land.

POM POM PRESS
Hackney Downs Studios
Charcoal Hall
Amhurst Terrace
London E8 2BT
United Kingdom

www.carbonbalancedpaper.com
CBP00019082504183028

Stay in Touch:
pompommag.com

 @pompommag

 @pompommag

ravelry.com/groups/pom-pom

 @pompommag

 @pompommag

Contents

Mini Woodwardia
16

Mini Take Heart
28

Mini Shirley
36

Mini Lobelia
46

Pinwheel Blanket
54

Mini Kordy
64

Mini Norn
74

Mini Pom Scarf
84

Mini Battenberg
94

Mini Skipworth
104

Truffle
112

To download your
free digital edition
of this book, please see
the download code
printed on the inside
of the back cover.

Introduction

It's no secret that babies love to be held. (It's not so bad holding a baby, either). As children grow, very gradually, so does the distance between them and their loved ones' arms, but connection is something they'll always need, even as big kids. We find knitting for kids (or anyone) is just an extension of that connection; that need to be held and comforted. Making something by hand that will keep them warm and snug is an incredible gesture of love that we're certain they can feel every time they're wrapped up in a blanket or garment of your creation.

Now, if this love-imbued creation of yours is also super fun and cute, maybe even a little functional? All the better! In *Mini Pom*, we've packed all of that into 11 versatile patterns, many of which are little versions of the grown-up designs we've published in our magazines and books over the last 10 years. We've added a few specifically kid-friendly designs into the mix too. Each of these patterns has been chosen and designed with little growing bodies and the way they move in mind.

We hope these designs bring you and the young people you knit them for years of joy and cosy memories! We feel all warm and fuzzy just thinking about it.

Lots of woolly love,
Meghan + Lydia
xoxo

Knitting for Kids:
Tips + Tricks

Kids are energetic and are getting to know their senses every day. They are often moving, swinging, jumping, and figuring out where their bodies are in space and what they can do. Kids are messy and growing and changing all the time. How on earth do we knit for these dynamic little creatures? We've amassed a wealth of knowledge on this very topic and offer the following suggestions and advice to consider before you embark on hours of stitching.

Choosing a Pattern

First things first, you will need to choose a design to make for a little one. Which little one you're knitting for is key. Knitting for a baby is easy. They're usually happy with anything that will keep them warm and don't have many opinions on the subject yet. Their parents will discover that they can't have too many baby blankets to cover them on walks, or to play on at home. Socks are something that newborns also seem to need in endless supply. Even in summer, babies' circulatory systems aren't quite up to scratch yet, and their toes can always use some extra warmth. And in terms of garments, cardigans are the easiest for getting on and off wiggly arms that don't know where to go yet, and avoid the struggle of tugging a pullover over a baby's head. That said, we've made sure the neck openings for each of the pullovers in this book are plenty generous. If you're knitting for a baby or parent whose tastes you're not too sure of, a cuddly soft toy might be just the thing, and our pal Truffle the pig is a proven favourite with kids of all ages.

Older kids will have more thoughts and opinions on what they would like to wear (and fair enough!). Now would be a great time to get them involved in the process and become invested in the finished product. Children love being asked their favourite colour (we know more than one who will say "rainbow!") and we're sure they'll enjoy flipping through these pages in order to choose their favourite designs.

Choosing Yarns

Kids are messy, like, really messy. They like to play in dirt, they get sand in their shoes, they haven't quite figured out that napkins are a better choice than their clothes when they eat. And that's if all the food actually makes it into their mouths. You will spend precious many hours knitting for them, so it's best to keep all this in mind when choosing yarns. The yarns featured in this book work brilliantly for their respective patterns and we love them, but they are not the only options! We frequently substitute yarns when making patterns for ourselves and encourage you to try other options for your lucky little recipients too, especially yarns already in your stash. There can be lots of reasons for using a different yarn to the one listed in the pattern; prices vary, and some yarns aren't easy to obtain because they are dyed or produced in very small batches, or perhaps because they aren't local to you.

There are three main things to consider when choosing or substituting yarns for little knits:

- **Durability**   - **Washability**   - **Wearability (or softness)**

In terms of durability, a beautiful cashmere yarn might be lovely for small babies who don't move around much and aren't in much danger of snagging it in the playground. But keep in mind they do tend to regurgitate milk with no notice so weigh up your cashmere decisions carefully! (And maybe pair the garment with a bib.)

Older children who move about much more will probably need sturdier yarns. Wool can be immensely strong and forgiving (it spent a while on a dirty sheep so can probably handle a kid too), but you'll want to balance the durability with softness - generally the softer a wool is, the less durable it will be. Softer wools are prone to pilling, too.

Because they can be so messy, kids' knitwear will probably need more washing than an adult's. There are treated, 'superwash' wools that can be put in a washing machine but beware: it needs to be a gentle, cold wash and a low setting in a dryer. Superwash wools are not the most ecologically friendly either, so keep the preferences of the adult who will be doing the washing in mind.

Top Tip! Helping Kids Choose a Design

Children have unlimited imaginations, but sometimes they need help knowing what's possible. When you show them the designs in this book, keep in mind they might not know that it can be made in whatever colour they choose, and worn with whatever clothes they have in their wardrobes. Or that the garment doesn't need to be worn by only babies, or only certain genders. You could show them yarns from your stash or take them to a yarn shop to get them excited about the possibilities.

For the designs in this book, we've provided colouring pages (see page 122) for kids to experiment with and make their own! You can also download and print these pages for lots of colour exploration. To take it to another level, print a photo of the child and cut out the piece of knitwear to play with like a paper doll! That's not only fun, but also a great way for them to visualise how it might actually look and feel on themselves.

Mini Pom

Untreated wools are the more eco-friendly choice, but will require handwashing and laying flat to dry. Be sure to make it very clear to the recipient's grown-ups how your knit is meant to be washed!

As practical as we're being here, we also know how heartbreaking it is to think about soiling, snags, and stretching when we're talking about a precious handknit that you'll spend hours working on. But we also know how fulfilling it is for a handknit to be worn and loved instead of sitting in a drawer; ultimately this is part of the joy of making! Also, by taking the time to make pragmatic choices about materials before you start, you're adding to the longevity of your project. A yarn that can stand up to more than one child's wear and washing could be lovingly passed on to siblings and friends.

Finally, it seems a cliché that children find homemade knitwear scratchy, but sometimes they really do! Children's skin can be more sensitive than many adults', and they are often hyper-aware of their senses (think loud fireworks in tiny ears), and some will have specific sensory needs. If you are making a gift it's probably wise to check in with the child's grown-up to make sure your yarn of choice will be wearable for the kiddo you have in mind. Cotton might be a good (and easy-wash) choice for kids who are particularly sensitive to wool and don't need as much warmth as animal fibres provide. Although most garments will be layered over other pieces of clothing, keep in mind that especially sensitive spots, like necks and foreheads, often come into direct contact with collars and hat brims.

Choosing yarns can be daunting but if you keep this guidance in mind, you'll be on the right track. You'll also find specific yardage requirements listed within our patterns to help you decide exactly how much of an alternative yarn you will need. Be sure to consider the ratio of yarn ball length to the weight of the yarn listed, and look for something similar with your substitution. This means the number of metres/yards to grams/ounces. If your yarn's ratio is similar to that of the yarn called for in the pattern, your yarn will usually be the right thickness to get gauge. If you have any doubts when substituting, ask for help! We encourage you to engage with the expertise of your local yarn shop. You are also welcome to join our forum on Ravelry, where other Pom knitters and staff are always around to share ideas with, or reach out to us directly at *contact@pompommag.com*.

Choosing a Size

Children, like adults, come in all shapes and sizes regardless of their age. The patterns in this book offer approximate age brackets for each garment, but these are only guidelines. The best way to ensure a good fit for the kid you're knitting for is to measure them and then check the finished dimensions of the garment in the pattern. Keep in mind what season you are knitting for and when you intend them to wear it. If it is already winter and you want the child to wear the garment that season, hopefully you are a speedy knitter and the child won't grow too much before you are done. But if you are knitting in summer to prepare for the following winter, keep in mind that the child may grow before then! Knitting a size up is often the wisest choice - if the garment doesn't fit yet, it definitely will at some point in the future, or perhaps just fit a bit roomily for a while, but there's not a lot you can do with a garment that's already too small (except maybe pass it along to a younger sibling, or for dressing up a favourite toy).

Making Adjustments

All of the knit garments in this book are worked from the collar downwards, meaning the last things you do are the bottom hem and the cuffs of the sleeves. (The exception to this would be our crocheted cardigan, Battenberg, but we'll get to that in a moment). This is great news! What this means is that you can adjust the lengths to suit the child you are knitting for. Some kids are short and some are tall. You have control over how long you want your garments to be.

The other point to keep in mind is that of course kids grow. One day their sleeves will be the perfect length and the next day their hands will be inches beyond the cuffs! There are two solutions to this problem:

Knit sleeves longer than the child will need at first. Cuffs can be folded up for a while (you will see some of the little models in this book with that look) and unrolled as the child grows. As they grow, you can unravel the cuffs or hem and add length as needed! Just make sure you set aside any leftover yarn from the project for use later.

All of this applies to our crochet cardigan design, Battenberg, as well, except that in this case, to add length you can add another row of granny squares to the hem or sleeves as needed. You can also just add a few rows of single or double crochet stitches if you only need a bit of extra length.

Mini Pom

The Patterns

Mini Woodwardia

by Lydia Gluck

Possibly the most versatile of the designs in this book, *Woodwardia* works as a lovely canvas to play with colour or keep it simple depending on the family you're knitting for. The wonderful thing about kids' knits is that you don't need a lot of yarn to make a garment! Have two or three partial skeins of yarn left from another project? Try colour blocking! A lot of scraps? Stripes! Two sets of fine weight yarns? Try marling them. The subtle detail at the raglan seams can handle a bit of colourplay but equally shines in a solid shade.

#MiniWoodwardia

Sample 1 (Yellow version, shown here)
Royce (age 10 mths) and Lola (age 18 mths) are shown wearing a size 4.

Neighborhood Fiber Co. Organic Studio DK (DK-weight; 100% organic Merino wool; 251m / 275yds per 133g skein)

Shade: Penn North; 1 (2, 2, 2, 2, 2, 3, 3, 3) skeins

Gauge: 24 sts & 36 rows = 10cm / 4" over St st worked in the round on 3.5mm needles after blocking.

Needles: 3mm / US 2.5 circular needle, 40cm / 16" length AND needles suitable for working small circumferences in the round

3.5mm / US 4 circular needle, 40cm / 16" length AND 80cm / 32" length AND needles suitable for working small circumferences in the round

Always use a needle size that will result in the correct gauge after blocking.

Notions: 5 stitch markers (including one unique for beginning of round), scrap yarn or stitch holders, tapestry needle

Notes: *Mini Woodwardia* is worked top down in the round with raglan increases and optional short rows at the neck. At the underarm, sleeve stitches are put on hold and the body is worked in one piece, finishing with a split hem. The sleeve stitches are picked up and sleeves are worked down in the round. Finally, stitches are picked up around the neckline and a neckband is completed.
Adult version published in *Pom Pom Quarterly* Issue 28: Spring 2019 and *Ready Set Raglan*.

Sizes: 1 (2, 3, 4, 5, 6, 7, 8, 9)

To fit: 0-3 mths (3-6 mths, 6-12 mths, 12-18 mths, 1-2 yrs, 2-4 yrs, 4-6 yrs, 6-8 yrs, 8-10 yrs)

Finished chest (fullest point) circumference: 48.5 (51, 55, 56.5, 59, 63.5, 71.5, 76, 79)cm / 19 (20, 21½, 22½, 23¼, 25, 28, 30, 31¼)" - to be worn with up to 7.5cm / 3" positive ease.

Yarn: approximately 250 (290, 340, 400, 430, 490, 585, 700, 800)m / 273 (316, 371, 436, 469, 534, 638, 763, 872)yds of DK-weight yarn.

This sample of *Woodwardia* is a size up on Royce, shown on pages 19 and 20. We wanted to show how a larger size can work with the sleeves rolled up so that a child can wear the same pullover for multiple seasons!

Top Tip!

If you remember the orignal adult version of *Woodwardia* and your kiddo would like to replicate the cosy finish of the roll neck (turtleneck), simply knit to 15cm / 6" for the collar!

Stitch Glossary

2x2 Rib (worked in the round):
Worked over a multiple of 4 sts
Round 1: [K2, p2] to end.
Rep round 1 for patt.

2x2 Rib (worked flat):
Worked over a multiple of 4 sts + 2
Row 1 (WS): P2, [k2, p2] to end.
Row 2 (RS): K2, [p2, k2] to end.
Rep rows 1-2 for patt.

German Short Rows:
Create DS: Bring yarn to front, slip the first stitch as if to purl, bring yarn over the needle to the back of your work and pull tight (it will look like a double stitch = DS)
Resolving Double Stitches: When you encounter the DS on subsequent rows, work DS in pattern, inserting needle through both legs of the DS and treating it as one stitch.
See page 26 for our German Short Rows tutorial or *pompommag.com/tutorials.*

Sample 2 (Blue version, shown on pages 21 and 23)
Loden (age 5) is shown wearing a size 8.
Berroco Ultra Wool DK (DK-weight; 100% superwash Merino wool; 267m / 292yds per 100g balls)
Shade: Breeze (83163); 1 (2, 2, 2, 2, 3, 3, 3) balls

Pattern: Mini Woodwardia - Stocking Stitch Raglan with Decorative Increases

PATTERN BEGINS

Yoke

Using larger needles suitable for working small circumferences in the round and the long-tail method (page 44), cast on 74 (80, 84, 88, 92, 98, 98, 102, 104) sts. Join for working in the round being careful not to twist. PM to indicate beg of round at centre of right sleeve.

Set-up round: K5 (6, 5, 6, 7, 7, 5, 6, 7), PM, k27 (28, 31, 31, 32, 35, 39, 38, 38), PM, k10 (12, 11, 13, 14, 14, 10, 13, 14), PM, k27 (28, 31, 31, 32, 35, 39, 38, 38), PM, k5 (6, 6, 7, 7, 7, 5, 7, 7).

If working the straight neck version, proceed to **Straight Neck Yoke Shaping** instructions. If working the short row version proceed to **German Short Row Yoke Shaping** instructions.

Note: Change to longer circular needle when necessary as the yoke circumference increases.

Straight Neck Yoke Shaping

Round 1 (inc): [K to last st before marker, kfb, SM, kfb] four times, k to end. *8 sts inc*

Round 2: Knit.

Round 3 (inc): Rep round 1. *8 sts inc*

Round 4: [K to 3 sts before marker, p3, SM, k1, p3] four times, k to end.

Rounds 1-4 set raglan increase patt.

Rep rounds 1-4 a further 5 (6, 6, 7, 7, 7, 9, 10, 11) times, then repeat rounds 1-2 a further 1 (0, 1, 0, 0, 1, 0, 1, 1) times. *178 (192, 204, 216, 220, 234, 258, 286, 304) sts*

Proceed to BOTH versions

German Short Row Yoke Shaping

Short row 1 (RS): K to last st before marker, kfb, SM, kfb, k3, turn. *2 sts inc; 1 st on right sleeve, 1 st on front*

Short row 2 (WS): Create DS, p to beg of round marker, SM, [p to 2 sts before marker, pfb, p1, SM, pfb] 3 times, p3, turn. *6 sts inc, 1 st on right sleeve, 2 sts each on back and left sleeve, 1 st on front*

Short row 3: Create DS, k to beg of round marker, SM, k to last st before marker, kfb, SM, kfb, k to DS, resolve DS, k2, turn. *2 sts inc; 1 st on right sleeve, 1 st on front*

Short row 4: Create DS, p to 4 sts before marker, k3, p1, SM, k3, p to beg of round marker, SM, [p to 2 sts before marker, pfb, p1, SM, pfb] 3 times, p to DS, resolve DS, p2, turn. *6 sts inc; 1 st on right sleeve, 2 sts each on back and left sleeve, 1 st on front*

Short row 5: Create DS, [k to 3 sts before marker, p3, SM, k1, p3] 3 times, k to beg of round marker, SM, k to last st before marker, kfb, SM, kfb, k to DS, resolve DS, k2, turn. *2 sts inc; 1 st on right sleeve, 1 st on front*

Short row 6: Create DS, p to beg of round marker, SM, [p to 2 sts before marker, pfb, p1, SM, pfb] 3 times, p to DS, resolve DS, p2, turn. *6 sts inc; 1 st on right sleeve, 2 sts each on back and left sleeve, 1 st on front*

Short row 7: Create DS, k to beg of round marker, SM, k to last st before marker, kfb, SM, kfb, k to DS, resolve DS, k2, turn. *2 sts inc; 1 st on right sleeve, 1 st on front*

Short row 8: Create DS, p to 4 sts before marker, k3, p1, SM, k3, p to beg of round marker, SM, [p to 2 sts before marker, pfb, p1, SM, pfb] 3 times, p to DS, resolve DS, p2, turn. *6 sts inc; 1 st on right sleeve, 2 sts each on back and left sleeve, 1 st on front*

Sizes 1, 2, 3, 4 & 5 ONLY:

Short row 9 (RS): Create DS, [k to 3 sts before marker, p3, SM, k1, p3] three times, k to end. *106 (112, 116, 120, 124) sts*

Sizes 6, 7, 8 & 9 ONLY:

Rep Short rows 5-8 once more.

Short row 13 (RS): Create DS, [k to 3 sts before marker, p3, SM, k1, p3] 3 times, k to end. *146 (146, 150, 152) sts*

ALL sizes again

Work raglan increases as follows, resolving remaining DS as you pass them.

Round 1 (inc): [K to last st before marker, kfb, SM, kfb] four times, k to end. *8 sts inc*

Round 2: Knit.

Round 3 (inc): Rep round 1. *8 sts inc*

Round 4: [K to 3 sts before marker, p3, SM, k1, p3] four times, k to end.

Rounds 1-4 set raglan increase patt.

Rep rounds 1-4 a further 3 (4, 4, 5, 5, 4, 6, 7, 8) times, then repeat rows 1-2 a further 1 (0, 1, 0, 0, 1, 0, 1, 1) times. *178 (192, 204, 216, 220, 234, 258, 286, 304) sts*

BOTH versions

Work even in pattern, working purl sts at raglan markers every 4th round, until yoke measures 9.5 (10, 10.5, 11, 11, 13, 14.5, 16, 17)cm / 3¾ (4, 4¼, 4½, 4½, 5, 5¾, 6¼, 6¾)" from cast-on edge.

After yoke shaping is complete there will be 53 (56, 61, 63, 64, 69, 79, 84, 88) sts each for front and back, 36 (40, 41, 45, 46, 48, 50, 59, 64) sts each for sleeves.

Divide Body and Sleeves:

Next round: Remove beg of round marker, k to marker, SM, k to marker, remove marker, k1, place next 35 (39, 40, 44, 45, 47, 49, 58, 63) sts on holder for left sleeve, remove marker, using backwards-loop method cast on 2 (2, 2, 2, 3, 3, 3, 3, 3) sts, PM for left side "seam", cast on 2 (2, 2, 2, 3, 3, 3, 3, 3) sts, k to marker, remove marker, k1, place next 35 (39, 40, 44, 45, 47, 49, 58, 63) sts on holder for right sleeve, remove marker, using backwards-loop method cast on 2 (2, 2, 2, 3, 3, 3, 3, 3) sts, PM for new beg of round at right side "seam", cast on 2 (2, 2, 3, 3, 3, 3, 3) sts, k to left side "seam" marker, SM, k to end of round. *116 (122, 132, 136, 142, 152, 172, 182, 190) sts*

Body

Move beg of round marker 1 st to the left as follows: remove marker, sl1, replace marker for beg of round.
Now work body and establish garter "seam" as follows:

Round 1: K to 1 st before marker, p1, SM, p1, k to 2 sts before marker, p2.
Round 2: Knit.
Rep rounds 1-2 until piece measures 10 (11, 12.5, 13.5, 15, 16, 17.5, 20, 22.5)cm / 3¾ (4¼, 4¾, 5¼, 5¾, 6¼, 6¾, 7¾, 8¾)" from underarm or 3cm / 1¼" less than desired final length of front.

Split Hem

Move beg of round marker 1 st to the right as follows: remove marker, slip last st worked from RH needle to LH needle, replace marker for beg of round, slip st back to RH needle.
Next round: [K to marker and evenly dec 0 (3, 4, 2, 1, 2, 4, 1, 1) sts, SM] twice. *116 (116, 124, 132, 140, 148, 164, 180, 188) sts*
Change to smaller needles.
Split for hem as foll:

Front Hem

Row 1 (RS): [K2, p2] to last 2 sts before marker, k2, and turn, removing marker and leaving rem 58 (58, 62, 66, 70, 74, 82, 90, 94) sts on hold for Back Hem. *58 (58, 62, 66, 70, 74, 82, 90, 94) sts*
Row 2 (WS): Sl1 pwise wyif, p1, [k2, p2] to end.
Row 3: Sl1 pwise wyib, k1, [p2, k2] to end.
Rep rows 2-3 until front hem measures 3cm / 1¼", ending with a WS row.
Cast off loosely in rib.

Back Hem

With RS facing and smaller needles, return to held Back Hem sts. *58 (58, 62, 66, 70, 74, 82, 90, 94) sts*
Work as for Front Hem, repeating rows 2-3 until hem measures 5cm / 2", ending with a WS row.
Cast off loosely in rib.

Sleeves (both alike)

With RS facing, using larger needles suitable for working small circumferences in the round and beg at centre of underarm, pick up and knit 2 (2, 2, 2, 3, 3, 3, 3, 3) sts from underarm cast-on, knit across held sleeve sts, pick up and knit 2 (2, 2, 2, 3, 3, 3, 3, 3) sts from underarm cast-on, join to work in the round, PM for beg of round. *39 (43, 44, 48, 51, 53, 55, 64, 69) sts*
Dec round: K2tog, k to last 4 sts, ssk, PM, p2. *2 sts dec*
Next round: Knit.
Continue as set, maintaining garter stitch seam as for body, working in St st between markers and decreasing as set by Dec round every - (13, 25, 16, 14, 19, 20, 11, 13) rounds a further - (2, 1, 3, 4, 3, 4, 7, 7) times. *37 (37, 40, 40, 41, 45, 45, 48, 53) sts*
Note: The Dec round may sometimes be worked on a plain knit round.

Work straight, maintaining garter stitch seam as set, until sleeve measures 12.5 (13.5, 16, 20.5, 21.5, 23.5, 26, 28, 31) cm / 5 (5¼, 6¼, 8, 8½, 9¼, 10¼, 11, 12¼)" or 3cm / 1¼" less than desired length.

Sizes 1, 2, 5, 6, 7 & 9 ONLY:
Next round (dec): K to last 4 sts, ssk, PM, p2. *1 st dec, 36 (36, -, -, 40, 44, 44, -, 52) sts*

ALL sizes again
Cuff
Change to smaller needles.
Work in 2x2 Rib until cuff measures 3cm / 1¼".
Cast off loosely in rib.

Collar
With RS facing, using smaller 40cm / 16" circular needle and beg at centre of left shoulder, pick up and knit 74 (80, 84, 88, 92, 98, 98, 102, 104) sts around neckline. Join to work in the round, PM to indicate beg of round.
Knit one round and **at the same time** evenly dec 2 (-, -, -, -, 2, 2, 2, -) sts across the round. *72 (80, 84, 88, 92, 96, 96, 100, 104) sts*

Work in 2x2 Rib until collar measures 2cm / ¾" for short neckband or 15cm / 6" for roll neck (turtleneck).
Cast off loosely in rib.

FINISHING
Weave in ends and block to measurements.

a. Chest (fullest point) circumference: 48.5 (51, 55, 56.5, 59, 63.5, 71.5, 76, 79)cm / 19 (20, 21½, 22¼, 23¼, 25, 28, 30, 31¼)"
b. Length (front hem to underarm): 13 (14, 15.5, 16.5, 18, 19, 20.5, 23, 25.5)cm / 5 (5½, 6, 6½, 7, 7½, 8, 9, 10)"
c. Upper arm circumference: 16.5 (18, 19, 20, 21.5, 22, 23.5, 26.5, 29)cm / 6½ (7, 7½, 8, 8½, 8¾, 9¼, 10½, 11½)"
d. Yoke depth: 9.5 (10, 10.5, 11, 11, 13, 14.5, 16, 17)cm / 3¾ (4, 4¼, 4½, 4½, 5, 5¾, 6¼, 6¾)"
e. Cuff circumference: 15 (15, 16.5, 16.5, 16.5, 18.5, 20, 20, 21.5)cm / 6 (6, 6½, 6½, 6½, 7¼, 7¾, 7¾, 8½)"
f. Neck circumference: 31 (33.5, 35, 36.5, 38.5, 41, 41, 42.5, 43.5)cm / 12¼ (13¼, 13¾, 14½, 15, 16, 16, 16¾, 17)"
g. Sleeve length: 15.5 (16.5, 19, 23.5, 24.5, 26.5, 29, 31, 34)cm / 6 (6½, 7½, 9¼, 9½, 10½, 11½, 12¼, 13¼)"
h. Neck drop (optional short rows version): 2 (2, 2, 2, 2, 3.5, 3.5, 3.5, 3.5)cm / ¾ (¾, ¾, ¾, ¾, 1¼, 1¼, 1¼, 1¼)"

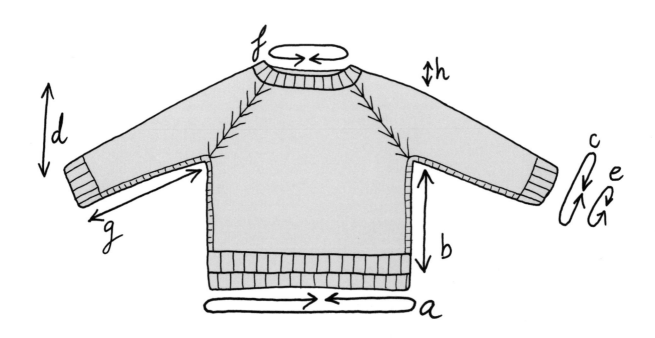

German Short Rows

Creating DS on RS

1. Work short row as instructed. Turn work so that the RS is facing.

2. Bring yarn to the front of work.

3. Slip one stitch purlwise to the right needle.

4. Pull working yarn tightly over the needle to back of work. This will make your stitch look like a double stitch (DS).

5. Knit the next stitch and continue working the short row as instructed.

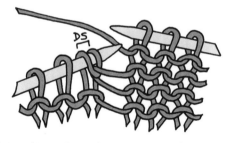

6. Resolving this DS from the WS: Your DS from the previous row will look like a double stitch.

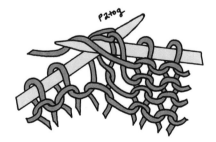

7. Purl both legs of DS together.

Mini Pom

Creating DS on WS

1. Work short row as instructed. Turn work so that the WS is facing.

2. Bring yarn to the front of work.

3. Slip one stitch purlwise to the right needle.

4. Pull working yarn tightly over the needle and bring it back to the front of work. This will make your stitch look like a double stitch (DS).

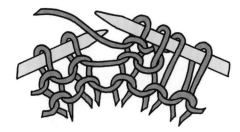

5. Purl the next stitch and continue working the short row as instructed.

6. Resolving this DS from the RS: Your DS from the previous row will look like a double stitch.

7. Knit both legs of DS together.

Mini
Take Heart

by Fiona Alice

The *Take Heart* design is one of the most beloved patterns in Pom Pom history! The genius use of cables to create a heart motif on the hat has captured many (non-knitted!) hearts over the years and we know kids will love this sweet but subtle touch. Our top tip for making this for the little ones in your life? Use a super soft yarn to ensure the hat feels comfortable on bare foreheads - we've found this area to be especially sensitive for babies and kids!

#MiniTakeHeart

Sizes: 1 (2, 3)

To fit: Baby (Toddler, Child)

Finished circumference: 37 (42.5, 46.5)cm / 14½ (16¾, 18¼)"

Yarn: approximately 125 (175, 200)m / 136 (190, 218)yds of DK-weight yarn

Sample 1 (Aqua version, shown on pages 28 and 31)

Royce (age 10 mths) and Sylvie (age 2) are shown wearing a size 2.

John Arbon Textiles Knit by Numbers DK (DK-weight; 100% Merino wool; 250m/273yds per 100g skein)

Shade: Aqua (KBN97); 1 skein

Gauge: 26.5 sts & 27 rows = 10cm / 4" over cable pattern on 4mm needles after blocking.

28 sts & 32 rows = 10cm / 4" over twisted ribbing on 3.5mm needle after blocking.

Needles: 3.5mm / US 4 circular needle, 40cm / 16" length 4mm / US 6 circular needle, 40cm / 16" length AND needles suitable for working small circumferences in the round Always use a needle size that will result in the correct gauge after blocking.

Notions: 1 stitch marker, cable needle, tapestry needle, 3.5 (4.5, 5)cm / 1½ (1¾, 2)" pompom maker (optional)

Notes: Hat is worked from the bottom up with long circular needles, using the Magic Loop method. A shorter circumference, like 40cm / 16", can be used instead for Size 2 & 3. However, DPNs will also be needed for working the decreases in the crown. Size 1 is too small for this method but can be worked just using DPNs.

The hat begins with the long-tail cast-on method (page 44) but a preferred stretchy cast on can be used instead. Adult version published in *Take Heart: A Transatlantic Knitting Journey.*

Stitch Glossary

1x1 Twisted Ribbing (in the round)

Round 1: [K1 tbl, p1 tbl] to end.

Rep round 1 for pattern.

1/1 RC: Sl 1 st to cable needle and hold at back, k1 from needle, k1 from cable needle.

2/2 LC: Sl 2 sts to cable needle and hold at front, k2 from needle, k2 from cable needle.

2/2 RC: Sl 2 sts to cable needle and hold at back, k2 from needle, k2 from cable needle.

2/1 LPC: Sl 2 sts to cable needle and hold at front, p1 from needle, k2 from cable needle.

2/1 RPC: Sl 1 st to cable needle and hold at back, k2 from needle, p1 from cable needle.

2/2 LPC: Sl 2 sts to cable needle and hold at front, p2 from needle, k2 from cable needle.

2/2 RPC: Sl 2 sts to cable needle and hold at back, k2 from needle, p2 from cable needle.

2/3 LPC: Sl 2 sts to cable needle and hold at front, p3 from needle, k2 from cable needle.

2/3 RPC: Sl 3 sts to cable needle and hold at back, k2 from needle, p3 from cable needle.

Mini Pom

WRITTEN INSTRUCTIONS FOR CHARTS

Worked over 24 (22, 24) sts

Round 1: 1/1 RC, p7 (6, 7), 2/2 RC, 2/2 LC, p7 (6, 7).

Round 2: K2, p7 (6, 7), k8, p7 (6, 7).

Round 3: 1/1 RC, p5 (4, 5), 2/2 RPC, k4, 2/2 LPC, p5 (4, 5).

Round 4: K2, p5 (4, 5), k2, p2, k4, p2, k2, p5 (4, 5).

Round 5: 1/1 RC, p4 (3, 4), 2/1 RPC, p2, 2/2 RC, p2, 2/1 LPC, p4 (3, 4).

Round 6: K2, p4 (3, 4), k2, p3, k4, p3, k2, p4 (3, 4).

Round 7: 1/1 RC, p4 (3, 4), k2, p3, k4, p3, k2, p4 (3, 4).

Round 8: Rep round 6.

Round 9: 1/1 RC, p4 (3, 4), 2/3 LPC, 2/2 RC, 2/3 RPC, p4 (3, 4).

Round 10: Rep round 2.

Sample 2 (Purple version, shown here and on page 35)
Sylvie (age 2) and Sabine (age 5) are shown wearing a size 3.

John Arbon Textiles Knit by Numbers DK (DK-weight; 100% Merino wool; 250m / 273yds per 100g skein)
Shade: Purple (KBN30); 1 skein

Sample 3 (Beige version, shown on page 30)
Sample shown is size 1.

John Arbon Textiles Knit by Numbers DK (DK-weight; 100% Merino wool; 250m / 273yds per 100g skein)
Shade: Beige (KBN115); 1 skein

Mini Pom

PATTERN BEGINS
BRIM
Using smaller circular needle and long-tail method, cast on 96 (110, 120) sts. Join for working in the round being careful not to twist. PM for beg of round.

Work in 1x1 Twisted Ribbing until brim measures 9 (9, 10)cm / 3½ (3½, 4)".

Set-up
Change to larger circular needles.
Round 1: [K2, p9 (8, 9), k4, p9 (8, 9)] to end.
Round 2: [1/1 RC, p9 (8, 9), k4, p9 (8, 9)] to end.
Round 3: Rep round 1.
Round 4: [1/1 RC, p9 (8, 9), 2/2 RC, p9 (8, 9)] to end.
Round 5: Rep round 1.

Commence Chart
Working from Chart or Written Instructions, work rounds 1-10 of Chart A a total of 2 (3, 4) times, working 24 (22, 24) st rep 4 (5, 5) times across round.

Sizes 1 & 3 ONLY
Next Round: [1/1 RC, p5, p2tog, 2/2 RC, 2/2 LC, p2tog, p5] to end. *88 (-, 110) sts*
Next Round: [K2, p6, k8, p6] to end.

Size 2 ONLY
Next Round: [1/1 RC, p6, 2/2 RC, 2/2 LC, p6] to end. *110 sts*
Next Round: [K2, p6, k8, p6] to end.

ALL sizes again
Crown Shaping
Change to needles for working small circumferences as required while decreasing.
Round 1: [1/1 RC, p2, p2tog, 2/2 RPC, k4, 2/2 LPC, p2tog, p2] to end. *80 (100, 100) sts*
Round 2: [K2, p3, k2, p2, k4, p2, k2, p3] to end.
Round 3: [1/1 RC, p2, 2/1 RPC, p2tog, 2/2 RC, p2tog, 2/1 LPC, p2] to end. *72 (90, 90) sts*
Round 4: [K2, p2, k2, p2, k4, p2, k2, p2] to end.

Round 5: [1/1 RC, p2, sl 2 sts to cable needle and hold in front, p2 from needle, ssk from cable needle, k4, sl 2 sts to cable needle and hold in back, k2tog from needle, p2 from cable needle, p2] to end. *64 (80, 80) sts*
Round 6: [K2, p4, k6, p4] to end.

Round 7: [K2tog, (p2tog) twice, k1, 2/2 RC, k1, (p2tog) twice] to end. *44 (55, 55) sts*
Round 8: [K1, p1, p2tog, k4, p2tog, p1] to end. *36 (45, 45) sts*
Round 9: [K1, p2, ssk, k2tog, p2] to end. *28 (35, 35) sts*
Round 10: [K1, p2tog, k2tog, p2tog] to end. *16 (20, 20) sts*

FINISHING
Break yarn leaving a 20cm / 8" tail. Thread tail through remaining sts, pull tight and secure. Weave in ends, block and leave to dry thoroughly. Attach pompom.

a. Finished circumference: 37 (42.5, 46.5)cm / 14½ (16¾, 18¼)"
b. Finished length: 18 (21.5, 26)cm / 7 (8½, 10¼)" with brim folded

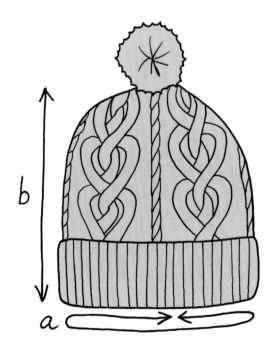

Chart A

| 24 | 23 | 22 | 21 | 20 | 19 | 18 | 17 | 16 | 15 | 14 | 13 | 12 | 11 | 10 | 9 | 8 | 7 | 6 | 5 | 4 | 3 | 2 | 1 | |

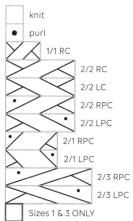

Key

	knit
•	purl
	1/1 RC
	2/2 RC
	2/2 LC
	2/2 RPC
	2/2 LPC
	2/1 RPC
	2/1 LPC
	2/3 RPC
	2/3 LPC
	Sizes 1 & 3 ONLY

Mini Shirley

by Rachel Coopey

For some reason, new babies need their feet kept warm more than anyone and yet they are the worst at keeping socks on! We modified the grown-up version of the *Shirley* socks, from our sock compendium, *Ready Set Socks*, to have a generous ankle length and fold-over cuff, which helps immensely with ensuring they stay snug! Not only practical, these socks also look super cool with their two-colour, mosaic stitch patterning, ensuring kiddos really start off on the right foot.

#MiniShirley

Mini Pom

Sizes: 1 (2, 3, 4, 5)
To fit foot circumference: 11.5 (14, 15, 16.5, 18)cm / 4½ (5½, 6, 6½, 7)" – to be worn with approx. 1.5cm / ½" negative ease
Foot length is fully adjustable within the pattern. Finished sock measures 0.5cm / ¼" less than actual foot length to ensure a good fit.
Yarn A: approximately 44 (66, 80, 116, 141)m / 48 (73, 88, 128, 155)yds of fingering / 4-ply-weight yarn
Yarn B: approximately 31 (47, 56, 82, 99)m / 34 (52, 62, 90, 109)yds of fingering / 4-ply-weight yarn
Yarn C: approximately 44 (66, 80, 116, 141)m / 48 (73, 88, 128, 155)yds of fingering / 4-ply-weight yarn

Sample 1 (Blue + pink version, shown here and on pages 36, 39, 40,and 43)
Sabine (age 5) and Loden (age 5) are shown wearing a size 4.
Retrosaria Mondim (fingering / 4-ply-weight; 100% fine Portuguese wool; 385m / 421yds per 100g ball)
Yarn A: 204; 1 ball
Yarn C: 204; 1 ball
Note: If using the same shade for Yarn A + C (as shown in sample 1) 1 ball is sufficient for all sizes.
John Arbon Textiles Devonia Minis 4ply (fingering / 4-ply-weight; 50% Exmoor Blueface, 30% Westcountry Bluefaced Leicester, 20% Westcountry lustre breeds; 97m / 106yds per 25g skein)
Yarn B: Dark Skies; 1 (1, 1, 2, 2) skeins
Gauge: 36 sts & 50 rounds = 10cm / 4" over St st on 2.5mm needles, after blocking
Needles: 2.5mm / US 1.5 needles suitable for working small circumferences in the round
Always use a needle size that will result in the correct gauge after blocking.
Notions: 2 stitch markers, tapestry needle
Notes: These socks are worked from the cuff down, with a ribbed cuff and a lace striped pattern on the leg and foot. Leg length is customisable by working fewer/more repeats. The heel is worked using the heel flap and gusset method. When changing yarns, ensure you twist the new colour with the previous colour between stripes to avoid holes. Take care not to pull yarns too tight between stripes to prevent the fabric from pulling.
Adult version published in *Ready Set Socks*.

Sample 2 (Green + pink version, shown on pages 38 and 41)
Sample shown is size 1.
Hedgehog Fibres Sock Minis (fingering / 4-ply-weight;
90% merino, 10% nylon; 80m / 87yds per 20g skein)
Yarn A: Beach Bunny; 1 (1, 2, 2, 2) skeins
Yarn B: Kelp; 1 (1, 1, 2, 2) skeins
Yarn C: Rosehip; 1 (1, 2, 2, 2) skeins

Note: sample 2 shows colours A and C reversed for
the second sock.

Pattern: Mini Shirley: Mosaic Stitch Socks

PATTERN BEGINS
SOCK ONE
CUFF

With yarn A, and using the long-tail method (page 44), cast on 40 (48, 52, 56, 60) sts. Join to work in the round, being careful not to twist sts. PM for beg of round.
Rib round: *P2, k2; rep from * to end.
Rep last round a further 29 times. Break yarn A.

LEG

Change to yarn B. Knit 2 rounds.
Join yarn C and begin working in lace stripe pattern as foll:
Round 1: With yarn C, knit.
Round 2: With yarn C, *k2, yo, ssk; rep from * to end.
Round 3: With yarn B, *k3, sl1 wyib; rep from * to end.
Round 4: With yarn B, knit.
Round 5: With yarn C, knit.
Round 6: With yarn C, *yo, ssk, k2; rep from * to end.
Round 7: With yarn B, *k1, sl1 wyib, k2; rep from * to end.
Round 8: With yarn B, knit.
Last 8 rounds set lace stripe patt. Rep rounds 1-8 a further 0 (0, 0, 0, 1) times, then work rounds 1-4 only once more.

HEEL

Heel Flap:

Turn work so WS is facing. Heel flap will be worked back and forth on the next 20 (24, 26, 28, 30) sts with yarn A, beg with a WS row. Keep rem 20 (24, 26, 28, 30) sts on needles for instep.
Change to yarn A.
Row 1 (WS): Sl1 wyif, p19 (23, 25, 27, 29).
Row 2 (RS): *Sl1 wyib, k1; rep from * to end.
Rep rows 1-2 a further 9 (11, 12, 13, 14) times, then work row 1 only once more.

Heel Turn:
Row 1 (RS): Sl1 wyib, k10 (12, 14, 14, 16), ssk, k1, turn, leaving rem 6 (8, 8, 10, 10) sts unworked. *1 st dec*
Row 2 (WS): Sl1 wyif, p3 (3, 5, 5, 5), p2tog, p1, turn, leaving rem 6 (6, 8, 10, 10) sts unworked. *1 st dec*
Row 3: Sl1 wyib, k to 1 st before gap, ssk, k1, turn. *1 st dec*
Row 4: Sl1 wyif, p to 1 st before gap, p2tog, p1, turn. *1 st dec*
Rep rows 3-4 a further 2 (3, 3, 4, 4) times.
All heel sts have now been worked. *12 (14, 16, 16, 18) heel sts rem*

Gusset:

Begin working in the round again as foll:
Set-up round: With yarn C, sl1 wyib, k11 (13, 15, 15, 17), pick up and knit 10 (12, 13, 14, 15) sts along edge of heel flap (1 st in each slipped st along edge of flap), knit across 20 (24, 26, 28, 30) held instep sts, pick up and knit 10 (12, 13, 14, 15) sts along edge of heel flap, k22 (26, 29, 30, 33) sts, PM for beg of round at beg of instep sts. *52 (62, 68, 72, 78) sts*
Next round (dec): Work round 6 of lace stripe pattern across 20 (24, 26, 28, 30) sts, ssk, k to last 2 sts, k2tog. *2 sts dec*
Next round: With yarn B, work next round of lace stripe pattern across 20 (24, 26, 28, 30) sts, k to end.
Working next round of lace stripe pattern each time, changing colours as set by lace stripe pattern, rep last 2 rounds a further 5 (6, 7, 7, 8) times. *40 (48, 52, 56, 60) sts; 20 (24, 26, 28, 30) sts each on instep and sole*

FOOT

Work straight in patt as set, working lace stripe pattern on instep and St st on sole, until sock measures 7 (7, 8, 10, 12)cm / 2¾ (2¾, 3¼, 4, 4¾)" from back of heel or 3 (3.5, 3.5, 4, 4)cm / 1¼ (1½, 1½, 1½, 1½)" less than desired foot length, ending with a knit round.

TOE

Break yarn B and C. Continue with yarn A only.
Round 1: Knit.
Round 2 (dec): K1, ssk, k14 (18, 20, 22, 24), k2tog, k1, PM, k1, ssk, k to last 3 sts, k2tog, k1. *36 (44, 48, 52, 56) sts*
Round 3: Knit.
Round 4 (dec): *K1, ssk, k to 3 sts before marker, k2tog, k1, SM; rep from * once more. *4 sts dec*
Rep rounds 3-4 a further 5 (7, 7, 8, 8) times. *12 (12, 16, 16, 20) sts*
Break yarn, leaving a 30cm / 12" tail. Graft sts together.
See page 45 for our Grafting tutorial or pompommag.com/tutorials.

SOCK TWO
CUFF
Work as for Sock One, using remaining colours as desired.

LEG
Change to yarn B. Knit 2 rounds.
Join yarn C and begin working in lace stripe pattern as foll:

Round 1: With yarn C, knit.
Round 2: With yarn C, *k2, k2tog, yo; rep from * to end.
Round 3: With yarn B, *k2, sl1 wyib, k1; rep from * to end.
Round 4: With yarn B, knit.
Round 5: With yarn C, knit.
Round 6: With yarn C, *k2tog, yo, k2; rep from * to end.
Round 7: With yarn B, *sl1 wyib, k3; rep from * to end.
Round 8: With yarn B, knit.
Last 8 rounds set lace stripe patt. Rep rounds 1-8 a further 0 (0, 0, 0, 1) times, then work rounds 1-4 only once more.

HEEL, FOOT & TOE
Work as for Sock One.

FINISHING
Weave in ends and block to measurements.

a. Leg length (with ribbing folded in half): 6.5 (6.5, 6.5, 6.5, 7.5)cm / 2½ (2½, 2½, 2½, 3)"
b. Foot circumference (unstretched): 11 (13.5, 14.5, 15.5, 16.5) cm / 4¼ (5¼, 5¾, 6, 6½)"

LONG-TAIL CAST-ON

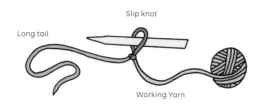

Long tail · Slip knot · Working Yarn

1. Make a slip knot leaving a generous tail and place on needle. Your tail will need to be at least 3 times the length of the project's finished measurement to make the required number of stitches.

2. Arrange yarn on left hand, with the long tail over thumb and the working yarn threaded behind index finger.

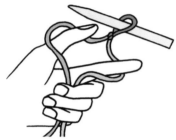

3. Bend fingers to trap the long tail and working yarn and hold secure.

4. Scoop needle from left to right to pick up tail yarn on left side of thumb.

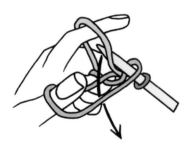

5. Lean needle to pick up working yarn looped over index finger.

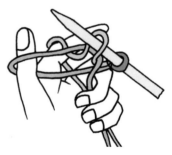

6. Draw working yarn through to create stitch on needle.

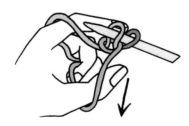

7. Make sure your new stitch is snug on the needle by gently pulling yarn tail with thumb in the direction shown. Don't pull too hard, you don't want your stitches to be too tight.

8. Ensure tail yarn and working yarn are arranged as detailed in Step 2 and repeat Steps 3 -7 to cast on required number of stitches.

GRATTING

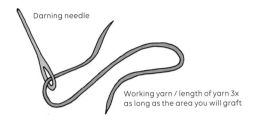

Darning needle

Working yarn / length of yarn 3x as long as the area you will graft

1. Thread your tapestry needle with working yarn or other length of yarn.

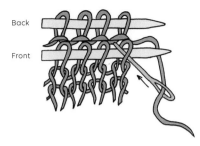

Back

Front

2. Arrange needles so they are parallel, with stitches at tip. Insert tapestry needle purlwise into first stitch on front needle and pull yarn through, leaving stitch on front needle.

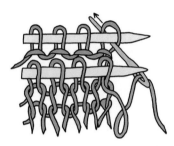

3. Insert tapestry needle knitwise into first stitch on back needle. Pull yarn through, leaving stitch on back needle.

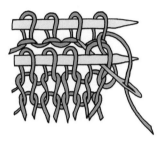

4. Insert tapestry needle knitwise into first stitch on front needle.

5. Slip this stitch off front needle. Enter next stitch purlwise and pull yarn through, leaving stitch on the front needle.

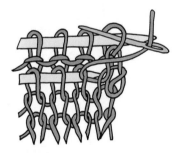

6. Insert tapestry needle purlwise into first stitch on back needle.

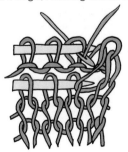

7. Slip this stitch off back needle. Enter next stitch knitwise and pull yarn through, leaving this stitch on back needle.

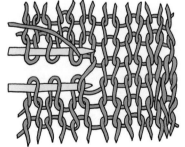

Adjust tension as you go

8. Repeat steps 4-7, weaving stitches together and adjusting tension as you go. Continue until one stitch is left on each needle. To finish, insert tapestry needle knitwise into stitch on front needle and slip off. Repeat purlwise on back needle and slip off. Adjust tension and weave in ends.

Mini Pom

Mini Lobelia

by Meghan Fernandes

Sure to please any mini floral aficionados, *Lobelia* makes use of the Estonian star flower motif often seen on exquisite lace shawls, but used here on a raglan cardigan. The flower motif is not exactly simple to work, but used sparingly it makes for an interesting but not overwhelming project. The effort put into those few but special flowers ensures this cardigan will be an heirloom for generations to come.

#MiniLobelia

Mini Pom

Gauge: 23 sts & 32 rows = 10cm / 4" in reverse St st using 3.75mm needles, after blocking.
Each flower motif measures 4.5cm / 1¾" wide & 2½ cm / 1" tall using 3.75mm needles.
Needles: 3.75mm / US 5 circular needle, 60cm / 24" length AND needles suitable for working small circumferences in the round.
3.25mm / US 3 circular needle, 60cm / 24" length AND needles suitable for working small circumferences in the round.
Always use a needle size that will result in the correct gauge after blocking.
Notions: 8 removable stitch markers, scrap yarn, 5 (5, 5, 5, 5, 7, 7, 9, 9) 1cm / 3/8" buttons
Notes: In a nod to the original pattern, (cropped cardigan with short sleeves) the body of this *Lobelia* is full length but the sleeves are bracelet length, finishing between 2.5cm and 5cm short of full length.
Adult cardigan version published in *Pom Pom Quarterly* Issue 4: Spring 2013. Adult pullover version published in *Ready Set Raglan*.

Stitch Glossary
1x1 Rib (worked flat):
Worked over an even number of sts
All rounds (RS): [K1, p1] to end.

1x1 Rib (worked in the round):
Worked over an even number of sts
All Rows: [K1, p1] to end.

3-into-9: *K3tog without dropping sts from left needle, yo; rep from * 4 times, k the same 3 sts tog once more, drop from left needle. 6 sts inc.

T3 (twist 3): Sl2 to cable needle, hold to back, k1tbl, sl 1st of held sts back to left needle, p this st, ktbl st from cable needle.

Flower Motif:
Row 1 (RS): P2, k3tog, 3-into-9, sssk, p2. *2 sts inc*
Row 2 (WS): K3, p9, k3.
Row 3: P1, p2tog, (yo, k3) 3 times, yo, p2tog tbl, p1. *2 sts inc*
Row 4: K3, (p3, k1) 3 times, k2.
Row 5: P3, yo, sssk, yo, p1, yo, k3, yo, p1, yo, k3tog, yo, p3. *2 sts inc*
Row 6: K8, p3, k8.
Row 7: P8, yo, s2kpo, yo, p8.
Row 8: K19.

Sizes: 1 (2, 3, 4, 5, 6, 7, 8, 9)
To fit: 0-3 mths (3-6 mths, 6-12 mths, 12-18 mths, 1-2 yrs, 2-4 yrs, 4-6 yrs, 6-8 yrs, 8-10 yrs)
Finished chest (fullest point) circumference (closed):
47 (50.5, 52.5, 56, 59.5, 63, 66.5, 71.5, 75)cm / 18½ (20, 20¾, 22, 23½, 24¾, 26¼, 25, 28¼, 29½)" - to be worn with up to 7.5cm / 3" positive ease.
Yarn: approximately 491 (527, 548, 584, 621, 658, 694, 746, 783)m / 537 (577, 600, 640, 680, 720, 760, 817, 857)yds of DK-weight yarn.
Sample (Pink, shown here)
Avienne (age 10) is wearing size 9.
Wandering Flock DK Merino (DK-weight; 100% superwash Merino wool; 211m / 231yds per 100g skein)
Shade: Electric Orchid; 3 (3, 3, 3, 4, 4, 4, 4) skeins

Cable Rib Pattern A (flat):
Worked over a multiple of 6 sts +1
Rows 1 & 5 (RS): K1tbl, *p1, k1tbl; rep from * to end.
Row 2, 4, 6 (WS): P1tbl, *k1, p1tbl; rep from * to end.
Row 3: K1tbl, *p1, T3, p1, k1tbl; rep from * to end.

Cable Rib Pattern B (in the round):
Worked over a multiple of 6 sts
Rounds 1, 2, 4, 5, 6: *K1tbl, p1; rep from * to end.
Round 3: *K1tbl, p1, T3, p1; rep from * to end.

PATTERN BEGINS
NECKLINE
With smaller needles, cast on 76 (84, 84, 88, 88, 92, 92, 100, 104) sts. Work in 1x1 Rib (worked flat) until Neckline measures 1.5cm / ½" ending with a RS row.
Change to larger needles.

Raglan Set-Up Row (WS): K5 (6, 6, 7, 7, 8, 8, 8, 10), PM, k13, PM, k0 (2, 2, 2, 2, 2, 2, 4, 4), PM, k13, PM, k14 (16, 16, 18, 18, 20, 20, 24, 24), PM, k13, PM, k0 (2, 2, 2, 2, 2, 2, 4, 4), PM, k13, PM, k5 (6, 6, 7, 7, 8, 8, 8, 10).

Raglan Shaping

Rows 1, 3, 5 & 7 (RS): [P to m, SM, work Flower Motif, SM] 4 times, p to end.

Rows 2, 4, 6 & 8: (WS): [K to m, SM, work Flower Motif, SM] 4 times, k to end.

Every full Flower Motif repeat adds 24 sts.

Rep Rows 1-8 a further 2 (3, 3, 3, 4, 4, 4, 5, 5) times, moving 1st, 3rd, 5th and 7th markers 3 sts to the left and 2nd, 4th, 6th and 8th markers 3 sts to the right before beg Row 1 of each rep. *148 (180, 180, 184, 208, 212, 212, 244, 248) sts*

Sizes 1, 7 & 9 ONLY:
Rep rows 1-4 only once more. *164 (228, 264) sts*

Sizes 3, 4, 6 & 8 ONLY:
Rep rows 1-2 only once more. *188 (192, 220, 252) sts*

ALL sizes again
Remove all markers.

Divide Body and Sleeves

Next row (RS): P23 (25, 26, 27, 29, 31, 32, 34, 37), place next 34 (38, 40, 40, 44, 46, 48, 54, 56) sts hold for left sleeve, cast on 4 (4, 4, 6, 6, 6, 8, 8, 8) sts, p50 (54, 56, 58, 62, 66, 68, 76, 78), place next 34 (38, 40, 40, 44, 46, 48, 54, 56) sts on hold for right sleeve, cast on 4 (4, 4, 6, 6, 6, 8, 8, 8) sts, p to end. *104 (112, 116, 124, 132, 140, 148, 160, 168) sts*

Work in Rev St st (p all sts on RS, k all sts on WS) until piece measures 10 (11, 12, 13.5, 14.5, 17.5, 19.5, 22.5, 25)cm / 4 (4¼, 4¾, 5¼, 5¾, 6¾, 7¾, 8¾, 9¾)" from underarm, or 3cm / 1¼" less than desired length, ending with a RS row.

Sizes 1, 2, 3, 4, 6, 7, & 8 ONLY:
Next row (WS): Knit, evenly decrease 1 (3, 1, 3, -, 1, 3, 3, -) sts across row. *103 (109, 115, 121, -, 139, 145, 157, -) sts*

Sizes 5 & 9 ONLY:
Next row (WS): K1, M1, k to end. *133 (169) sts*

ALL sizes again
Hem
Change to smaller needles.
Work rows 1-6 of Cable Rib Pattern A once, then work rows 1-4 once more.
Cast off loosely in patt using larger needles.

Sleeves (both alike)

Using larger needles suitable for working small circumferences in the round, with RS facing and beg at centre of underarm cast-on edge, pick up and purl 2 (2, 2, 3, 3, 3, 4, 4, 4) sts, p across held sleeve sts, pick up and purl 2 (2, 2, 3, 3, 3, 4, 4, 4) from cast-on underarm sts. PM to indicate beg of rnd. *38 (42, 44, 46, 50, 52, 56, 62, 64) sts*

Dec round: P2tog, p to last 2 sts, ssp. *2 sts dec*
Next round: Purl.

Continue as set, decreasing as set by Dec round every 7 (9, 7, 16, 9, 10, 9, 8, 8)th round a further 3 (2, 3, 1, 3, 4, 6, 6, 7) times. *30 (36, 36, 42, 42, 42, 42, 48, 48) sts*

Continue purling every round until sleeve measures 10 (11, 11, 12, 13, 18, 21, 23, 26)cm / 4 (4¼, 4¼, 4¾, 5, 7, 8¼, 9, 10¼)" or 3cm / 1¼" less than desired length.

Cuff
Change to smaller needles.
Work rounds 1-6 of Cable Rib Pattern B once, then work rounds 1-4 once more.
Cast off loosely in patt using larger needles.

FINISHING
Block cardigan to required measurements, pinning out the leaves of the flower motifs to open them up. Weave in ends when dry.

Left Buttonband:
With smaller needles and RS facing, pick up and knit about 54 (58, 62, 64, 72, 80, 88, 96, 104) sts evenly along Left Front edge of cardigan opening, picking up at a rate of 3 sts for every 4 rows. Exact st count is not important, but should be an even number.
Work in 1x1 Rib for 6 rows. Cast off loosely in patt using larger needles.

Mark button position for 5 (5, 5, 5, 5, 7, 7, 9, 9) buttonholes, evenly spaced along buttonband.

Right Buttonband:
With smaller needles and RS facing, pick up and knit sts evenly along Right Front edge to match Left Front.
Work in 1x1 Rib for 2 rows.
Row 3 (WS): Working in 1x1 Rib, add a yo to correspond to each marked button position, work in patt to end.
Row 4 (RS): Continuing to work in 1x1 Rib, when you come to a yo, work it tog with the foll st in patt.
Work 2 more rows in 1x1 Rib. Cast off loosely in patt using larger needles. Block again if desired.
Sew buttons to left button band to correspond with buttonholes on right button band.

a. Chest circumference (closed): 47.5 (51.5, 53, 56.5, 60, 64, 67, 72, 76)cm / 18¾ (20¼, 21, 22¼, 23¾, 25¼, 26½, 28½, 30)"

b. Length (hem to underarm): 13 (14, 15, 16.5, 17.5, 20.5, 22.5, 25.5, 28)cm / 5¼ (5½, 6, 6½, 7, 8, 9, 10, 11)"

c. Upper arm circumference: 16.5 (18, 19, 20, 21.5, 22.5, 24.5, 26, 27)cm / 6¼ (7, 7¼, 7½, 8¼, 8¾, 9½, 10½, 10¾)"

d. Yoke depth: 9.5 (10, 10.5, 10.5, 12.5, 13, 14.5, 15.5, 17)cm / 3¾ (4, 4¼, 4¼, 5, 5¼, 5¾, 6¼, 6¾)"

e. Cuff circumference: 13 (15.5, 15.5, 18, 18, 18, 18, 21, 21)cm / 5¼ (6, 6, 7, 7, 7, 7, 8¼, 8¼)"

f. Neck circumference (incl. button bands): 35.5 (38.5, 38.5, 40.5, 40.5, 42.5, 42.5, 46.5, 46.5)cm / 14 (15¼, 15¼, 16, 16, 16¾, 16¾, 18¼, 18¼)"

g. Sleeve length: 13 (14, 14, 15, 16, 21, 24, 26, 29)cm / 5¼ (5½, 5½, 6, 6¼, 8¼, 9½, 10¼, 11½)"

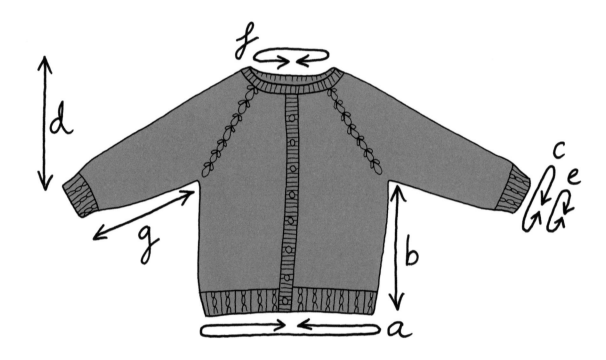

Chart

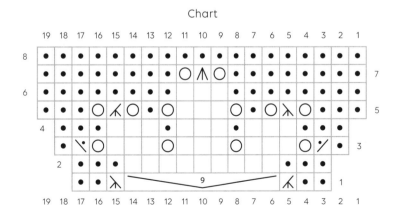

Key

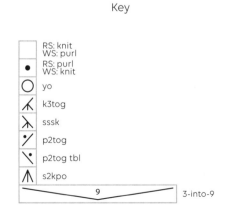

	RS: knit / WS: purl
•	RS: purl / WS: knit
O	yo
⋌	k3tog
⋋	sssk
⁄	p2tog
⧹	p2tog tbl
⋀	s2kpo

3-into-9

3 Into 9

1. This stitch takes place over the first three stitches on your left needle.

2. Insert right needle into these three stitches as if to knit.

3. Knit these three stitches together without dropping stitches from left needle. Make a yarn over.

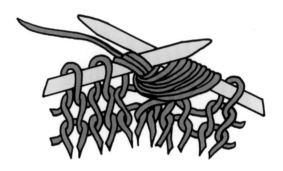

4. Repeat step 3 a further three times then knit the same three stitches once more.

5. Drop from left needle.

Top Tip!

The lacy Estonian Starflower pattern, especially the 3-into-9 stitch, is much easier to work with a sharp-tipped needle. If you find yourself struggling with blunter tips or wooden needles, it's time to try out some pointy metal tips.

Pinwheel Blanket

by Toshiyuki Shimada

Channelling the energy of whimsical and colourful pinwheels, this blanket is as lively as children themselves. Worked in an ingenious stitch pattern that uses colour blocking in entrelac motifs, this blanket would make the most unique of gifts to welcome a new human into the world. We've provided instructions for a large throw or a small pram-sized blanket, depending on your preference. And when the baby is a big kid? Use the pram-size as a super cute shawl for chilly days.

#MiniPinwheelBlanket

Mini Pom

OR
A total of approximately 460 (1250)m / 502 (1367)yds of fingering / 4-ply-weight yarn

Sample 1 (Small, 5-colour version, shown here and on pages 54, 58, 59 and 63)
Manos del Uruguay Alegria (fingering / 4-ply weight; 75% superwash Merino, 25% polyamide; 400m / 445yds per 100g skein)
Shades:
Yarn A: Sand (grey); 1 (3) skein(s)
Yarn B: Toy Soldier (green); 1 skein
Yarn C: Tumeria (yellow); 1 skein
Yarn D: Lavender (purple); 1 skein
Yarn E: Juanita (orange); 1 skein
Yarn F: Euphoria (pink); 1 skein
Gauge: 24 sts & 50 rows = 10cm / 4" in garter stitch using 3mm needles, after blocking
Needles: 3mm / US 2.5 needles, 60-80cm / 24-32" length
Always use a needle size that will result in the correct gauge after blocking.
Notions: Locking stitch marker, tapestry needle
Notes: Odd-numbered tiers are worked from right to left and consist of knit rows, while even-numbered tiers are worked from left to right and consist of purl rows.
There are 8 (10) garter ridges on the RS of each square.
If changing colours, join new colour after 4 (5) ridges on WS for WS squares and RS for RS squares.

Sizes: Small Blanket (Large Blanket)
Finished measurement: 49.5 (77)cm / 19½ (30¼)" wide, 40.5 (66)cm / 16 (26)" deep
Yarn A: approximately 375 (970)m / 409 (1057)yds of fingering / 4-ply-weight yarn
Yarn B: approximately 19 (56)m / 21 (62)yds of fingering / 4-ply-weight yarn
Yarn C: approximately 14 (56)m / 15 (62)yds of fingering / 4-ply-weight yarn
Yarn D: approximately 19 (56)m / 21 (62)yds of fingering / 4-ply-weight yarn
Yarn E: approximately 14 (56)m / 15 (62)yds of fingering / 4-ply-weight yarn
Yarn F: approximately 19 (56)m / 21 (62)yds of fingering / 4-ply-weight yarn

Mini Pom

Mini Pom

Stitch Glossary

LH Beg Square

Using the backwards-loop method, cast on 9 (11) sts, turn.

Row 1 (WS): P8 (10), p2tog (joining the last st with the first st of the adjoining Tier 1 motif), turn.

Row 2 (RS): P9 (11), turn.

Row 3 (WS): Sl1 pwise wyif, p7 (9), p2tog, turn.

Rep rows 2-3 a further 7 (9) times. Do not turn after last WS row.

Tier 2 WS Squares

Pick-up Row (WS): *With WS facing, insert RH needle tip into side edge of motif from back to front, wrap yarn as if to purl, draw st through to back; rep from * a further 7 (9) times, pick up loose strand between motifs with LH needle, p2tog strand with first st from adjacent Tier 1 motif, turn. *9 (11) sts*

Row 1 (RS): P9 (11), turn.

Row 2 (WS): Sl1 pwise wyif, p7 (9), p2tog, turn.

Row 3 (RS): P9 (11), turn.

Rep rows 2-3 a further 2 (3) times.

Change colours as necessary, rep rows 2-3 a further 3 (4) times, then work row 2 once more. Do not turn after last WS row.

Note: For a smooth transition, work the last st of the RS row before the colour change in the new colour. This stitch will be slipped at the beg of the next WS row.

WS Squares

Pick-up Row (WS): Pick up and purl 9 (11) sts evenly along edge of square, sl1 picked up st from RH needle to LH needle, p2tog, turn. *9 (11) sts*

Row 1 (RS): P9 (11), turn.

Row 2 (WS): Sl1 pwise wyif, p7 (9), p2tog, turn.

Row 3 (RS): P9 (11), turn.

Rep rows 2-3 a further 2 (3) times.

Change colours as necessary, rep rows 2-3 a further 3 (4) times, then work row 2 once more. Do not turn after last WS row.

RH End Square

Row 1 (WS): Pick up and purl 9 (11) sts evenly along edge of square, turn. *9 (11) sts*

Row 2 (RS): P9 (11), turn.

Row 3 (WS): Sl1 pwise wyif, p8 (10), turn.

Row 4 (RS): P9 (11), turn.

Rep rows 3-4 a further 6 (8) times, then work row 3 once more.

First RS Square

Pick-up Row (RS): There will remain 1 st on the RH needle. Pick up and knit 1 st close to the corner, pass 1 st over and off needle. Pick up and knit a further 8 (10) sts from edge of motif, sl1 kwise from adjoining motif, k2tog tbl the last 2 sts worked, turn. *9 (11) sts*

Row 1 (WS): K9 (11), turn.

Row 2 (RS): K8 (10), ssk last st with first st of adjoining tier, turn.

Rep rows 1-2 a further 7 (9) times. Do not turn after last RS row.

Remaining RS Squares

Pick-up Row (RS): Pick up and knit 9 (11) sts evenly along edge of square, sl1 kwise from adjoining motif, k2tog tbl the last 2 sts worked, turn. *9 (11) sts*

Row 1 (WS): K9 (11), turn.

Row 2 (RS): K8 (10), ssk last st with first st of adjoining tier, turn.

Row 3 (WS): K9 (11), turn.

Rep rows 2-3 a further 2 (3) times.

Change colours as necessary, rep rows 2-3 a further 4 (5) times, then work row 2 once more. Do not turn after last RS row.

NOTE: Colour changes occur on RS and WS squares only. Their position is noted, however use schematic as reference for colour placement.

Sample 2 (Large, 3-colour version, shown on page 61)

RAUMA Finull (sport / 4-ply-weight; 100% Norwegian wool; 175m / 191yds per 50g skein)

Shades:

Yarn A: 401 White; 3 (6) skeins

Yarn B: 458 Green; 1 skein

Yarn C: 478 Pink; 1 skein

OR approximately

Yarn A: 375 (950)m / 404 (1036)yds of fingering / 4-ply-weight yarn

Yarn B: 50 (125)m / 55 (136)yds of fingering / 4-ply-weight yarn

Yarn C: 30 (80)m / 33 (83)yds of fingering / 4-ply-weight yarn

Mini Pom

PATTERN BEGINS
Tier 1
*Using yarn A and the backwards-loop method, cast on 9 (11) sts.

Row 1 (WS): K9 (11), turn.
Row 2 (RS): K9 (11), turn.
Row 3 (WS): Sl1 kwise wyib, k8 (10), turn.
Row 4 (RS): K9 (11), turn.
Rep rows 3-4 a further 6 (8) times. Do not turn after last row 4.*
Place a locking marker into work to indicate RS.
Rep from * to * a further 10 (13) times. *11 (14) sets of 9 (11) sts on the needle*

Tier 2
With yarn A, work LH Beg Square once. Changing colours as indicated in schematic, work 10 (13) Tier 2 WS Squares.
With yarn A, work RH End Square once.
Cast off 8 (10) sts purlwise. *1 st rem on RH needle*

Tier 3
Changing colours as indicated in schematic, work one First RS Square, then 9 (12) Remaining RS Squares.

Tier 4
With yarn A, work LH Beg Square once. Changing colours as indicated in schematic, work 10 (13) WS Squares. With yarn A, work RH End Square once.
Cast off 8 (10) sts purlwise. *1 st rem on RH needle*

Blanket Body
Rep Tier 3 and Tier 4 a further 6 (9) times.

Final Tier Squares
**Pick-up Row (RS): There will remain 1 st on the RH needle. Pick up and knit a further 8 (10) sts from edge of motif, sl1 kwise from adjoining motif, k2tog tbl the last 2 sts worked, turn. *9 (11) sts*
Row 1 (WS): K9 (11), turn.
Row 2 (RS): K8 (10), ssk last st with first st of adjoining tier, turn.
Row 3 (WS): K9 (11), turn.

Rep rows 2-3 a further 6 (8) times.
Cast off 7 (9) sts, p2tog (1 st from square with 1 st from adjoining motif), pass 1 st over and off needle. *1 st rem***
Rep from ** to ** a further 9 (12) times.
Fasten off.

FINISHING
Weave in ends and block to measurements.

a. Finished width: 49.5 (77)cm / 19½ (30¼)"
b. Finished depth: 40.5 (66)cm / 16 (26)"

Note: Schematic shown denotes motif placement for the small blanket. The large blanket has one additional motif repeat both width and depth-wise.

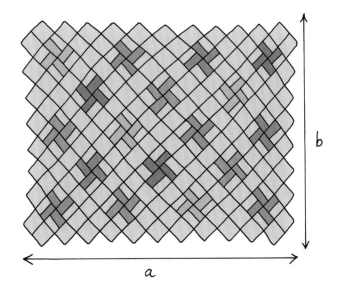

Mini
Kordy

by Kiyomi Burgin + Sachiko Burgin

Colouring pages are a childhood classic and this
is all that fun in pullover form! This is a great pattern
to get kids involved - have them grab their crayons and
go to town on our downloadable template (see pg 127).
As with cooking, the more a child is involved in the process,
the more likely they are to enjoy the finished product.
Kids' senses of colour are also much freer from the
constraints of socialised colour preferences - their choices
and combinations are sure to surprise and delight!

#MiniKordy

Sizes: 1 (2, 3, 4, 5, 6, 7, 8, 9)

To fit: 0-3 mths (3-6 mths, 6-12 mths, 12-18 mths, 1-2 yrs, 2-4 yrs, 4-6 yrs, 6-8 yrs, 8-10 yrs)

Finished chest (fullest point) circumference: 44 (47, 49, 52, 54, 58, 62, 65, 69)cm / 17¼ (18½, 19¼, 20½, 21¼, 22¾, 24½, 25½, 27¼)" – to be worn with approx 7.5cm / 3" positive ease

Yarn A: approximately 220 (255, 290, 330, 380, 460, 540, 630, 680)m / 245 (280, 320, 360, 420, 505, 595, 690, 750)yds of worsted-weight yarn

Yarn B: approximately 50 (50, 55, 55, 70, 75, 80, 85, 90)m / 55 (55, 60, 60, 75, 80, 85, 95, 100)yds of worsted-weight yarn

Yarn C: approximately 80 (80, 85, 90, 105, 110, 120, 125, 130)m / 90 (90, 95, 100, 115, 120, 130, 140, 145)yds of worsted-weight yarn

Yarn D: approximately 30 (30, 35, 35, 50, 50, 55, 65, 65)m / 35 (35, 40, 40, 55, 55, 60, 70, 70)yds of worsted-weight yarn

Sample (Yellow, shown here)
Sabine (age 5) and Avienne (age 10) are shown wearing a size 7.

Kelbourne Woolens Germantown (worsted-weight; 100% North American wool; 201m / 220yds per 100g skein)

Yarn A: 735 Yellow; 2 (2, 2, 2, 2, 3, 3, 3, 4, 4) skeins
Yarn B: 667 Salmon; 1 skein
Yarn C: 338 Jade; 1 skein
Yarn D: 105 Natural; 1 skein

Gauge: 20 sts & 27 rounds = 10cm / 4" over St st worked in the round on 4mm needles after blocking.

Needles: 4mm / US 6 circular needle, 40-60cm / 16-24" length (depending on size worked) AND needles suitable for working small circumferences in the round 3.75mm / US 5 circular needle, 40-60cm / 16-24" length (depending on size worked) AND needles suitable for working small circumferences in the round.

Note: Begin the yoke using needles suitable for working small circumferences in the round, then change to circular needles as the circumference increases. Always use a needle/hook size that will result in the correct gauge after blocking.

Notions: Stitch markers (2), spare DPN (for sizes 1-4), tapestry needle, one 10-12mm button (sizes 1-4 only)

Notes: *Mini Kordy* is worked from the top down almost entirely in the round, except for one small section that is worked back and forth to shape back. The first four smallest sizes have a split neck that fastens with a button at the left side to help make it a bit easier to get over little heads.

Adult version published in *Moon and Turtle: Knitting Patterns with Variations*

Stitch Glossary
2x2 Rib (in the round):
Round 1: [K2, p2] to end.
Rep round 1 for pattern.

PATTERN BEGINS

Sizes 1, 2, 3 & 4 ONLY

Using smaller needle in your preferred style for working small circumferences, yarn C, and the long-tail method (page 44), cast on 60 (60, 64, 64) sts. Do not join for working in the round.

Row 1 (WS): P3, [k2, p2] to last st, p1.
Row 2 (RS): K3, [p2, k2] to last st, k1.
Row 3 (buttonhole): P2tog, yo, p1, [k2, p2] to last st, p1.
Row 4 (RS): K3, [p2, k2] to last st, k1.
Row 5 (WS): P3, [k2, p2] to last st, p1.

Next row (RS): Slip the last 3 sts of row onto a spare DPN, join in the round by bringing those 3 last sts to lay on top of the first 3 sts of row (working yarn is at the back and the buttonhole is on top). [K2tog 1 st from front needle with 1 st from back needle] 3 times, p2, k2, PM to indicate beg of round. *57 (57, 61, 61) sts*
Next round: Knit, evenly inc 3 sts. *60 (60, 64, 64) sts*
Continue to ALL sizes again.

Sizes 5, 6, 7, 8 & 9 ONLY

Using smaller needle in your preferred style for working small circumferences, yarn C, and the long-tail method, cast on 68 (68, 72, 72, 72) sts. Join for working in the round being careful not to twist. PM to indicate beg of round.

Work in 2x2 Rib until neck measures 2.5cm / 1" from cast on edge.

ALL sizes again
Change to larger needles.
Increase Round:
Sizes 1, 4 & 9 ONLY: [K3 (4, 3), M1L] to end.
Sizes 2 & 3 ONLY: [K2, M1L] 6 (4) times, [k3, M1L] 12 (16) times, [k2, M1L] 6 (4) times.
Sizes 5, 6, 7 & 8 ONLY: [K3, M1L] 6 (6, 4, 4) times, [k4, M1L] 8 (8, 12, 12) times, [k3, M1L] 6 (6, 4, 4) times.
80 (84, 88, 80, 88, 88, 92, 92, 96) sts

Commence Chart

Begin chart specific to your size, working each round from right to left, joining new colours as necessary, working increases where indicated, and working 4-st rep 20 (21, 22, 20, 22, 22, 23, 23, 24) times across round. *140 (147, 154, 160, 176, 176, 184, 184, 192) sts*
Cut yarn C, continue with yarn A only.

Next round: Knit, inc 0 (3, 4, 8, 4, 4, 8, 6, 10) sts evenly. *140 (150, 158, 168, 180, 180, 192, 190, 202) sts*
Work even in St st until yoke measures 12 (12.5, 12.5, 13.5, 14, 14.5, 15, 15, 15.5)cm / 4¾ (5, 5, 5¼, 5½, 5¾, 6, 6, 6)" from bottom of ribbing.

Back Gusset

Next round: K40 (43, 44, 47, 50, 52, 56, 56, 60) sts for back, then place rem sts of round on 3 separate pieces of waste yarn in the following order: 30 (32, 35, 37, 40, 38, 40, 39, 41) sts for right sleeve, k40 (43, 44, 47, 50, 52, 56, 56, 60) sts for front, and 30 (32, 35, 37, 40, 38, 40, 39, 41) sts for left sleeve.

Working back and forth in St st over back sts only, work 3 (3, 3, 3, 3, 5, 5, 5, 5) rows, ending with a WS row.

Divide Body and Sleeves

Next round (RS): K40 (43, 44, 47, 50, 52, 56, 56, 60) sts for back, then using the backwards-loop method, cast on 4 (4, 5, 5, 4, 6, 6, 9, 9) sts for right underarm, leave next 30 (32, 35, 37, 40, 38, 40, 39, 41) sts for right sleeve on waste yarn, but transfer next 40 (43, 44, 47, 50, 52, 56, 56, 60) sts for front onto needle, and knit across these sts, leave next 30 (32, 35, 37, 40, 38, 40, 39, 41) sts for left sleeve on waste yarn, then using the backwards-loop method, cast on 4 (4, 5, 5, 4, 6, 6, 9, 9) sts for left underarm placing a marker for beg of round after 2 (2, 3, 3, 2, 3, 3, 5, 5) sts, and rejoin work in round. Knit one round to beg of round marker. *88 (94, 98, 104, 108, 116, 124, 130, 138) sts*

Work even in St st in the round until body measures 10 (12.5, 13.5, 15, 15, 16.5, 19, 21.5, 24)cm / 4 (5, 5¼, 6, 6, 6½, 7½, 8½, 9½)" from underarm, or 2.5 (2.5, 2.5, 2.5, 4, 4, 4, 4, 4)cm / 1 (1, 1, 1, 1½, 1½, 1½, 1½, 1½)" less than desired finished length.

Sizes 2, 3, 8 & 9 ONLY: Knit, dec 2 sts evenly. *92 (96, 128, 136) sts*

ALL sizes again

Hem

Change to smaller circular needle and work in 2x2 Rib until hem measures 2.5 (2.5, 2.5, 2.5, 4, 4, 4, 4, 4)cm / 1 (1, 1, 1, 1½, 1½, 1½, 1½, 1½)". Cast off loosely in patt.

Right Sleeve

Using larger needle in your preferred style for working small circumferences, return 30 (32, 35, 37, 40, 38, 40, 39, 41) sts for right sleeve back onto needle. Join yarn A near centre of underarm, and pick up and knit 2 (2, 2, 2, 2, 3, 3, 4, 4) st(s) along left half of underarm edge, then pick up and knit 4 (4, 4, 4, 4, 6, 6, 6, 6) sts along side of back gusset, k30 (32, 34, 36, 40, 38, 40, 36, 38) sleeve sts, pick up and knit 1 st in the gap at side, then pick up and knit 2 (2, 3, 3, 2, 3, 3, 5, 5) sts along right half of underarm edge back to centre. PM to mark beg of round. *39 (41, 45, 47, 49, 51, 53, 55, 57) sts*

Next round: Knit to last 3 (3, 4, 4, 3, 4, 4, 6, 6) sts, ssk, k to end. *38 (40, 44, 46, 48, 50, 52, 54, 55) sts*

Shape Sleeve

Work 3 (3, 3, 3, 4, 4, 4, 5, 5) rounds even in St st.

Dec round: K1, k2tog, knit to last 3 sts,, ssk, k1. *2 sts dec*
Rep Dec round every following 4 (4, 4, 5, 5, 5, 6, 6)th round a further 6 (5, 7, 8, 7, 8, 9, 8, 9) times. *24 (28, 28, 28, 32, 32, 32, 36, 36) sts*

Work even in St st until sleeve measures 11.5 (12.5, 14, 15, 16, 17, 19, 21.5, 24)cm / 4½ (5 (5½, 6, 6¼, 6¾, 7½, 8½, 9½)" from underarm, or 2.5 (2.5, 2.5, 2.5, 3, 3, 4, 4, 4)cm / 1 (1, 1, 1, 1¼, 1¼, 1½, 1½, 1½)" less than desired finished length.

Cuff

Change to smaller needle in your preferred style for working small circumferences for next round.
Work in 2x2 Rib until cuff measures 2.5 (2.5, 2.5, 2.5, 3, 3, 4, 4, 4)cm / 1 (1, 1, 1, 1¼, 1¼, 1½, 1½, 1½)". Cast off loosely in patt.

Left Sleeve

Using larger needle in your preferred style for working small circumferences, return 30 (32, 35, 37, 40, 38, 40, 39, 41) sts for left sleeve back onto needle. Join yarn A near centre of underarm, and pick up and knit 2 (2, 3, 3, 2, 3, 3, 5, 5) sts along left half of underarm edge, pick up and knit 1 st in gap at side, k30 (32, 35, 37, 40, 38, 40, 39, 41) sleeve sts, then pick up and knit 4 (4, 4, 4, 4, 6, 6, 6, 6) sts along side of back gusset, then pick up and knit 2 (2, 2, 2, 2, 3, 3, 4, 4) st(s) along right half of underarm edge to centre. PM to mark beg of round. *39 (41, 45, 47, 49, 51, 53, 55, 57) sts*

Next round: K2 (2, 2, 2, 2, 3, 3, 4, 4), k2tog, k to end. *38 (40, 44, 46, 48, 50, 52, 54, 55) sts*
Work as for Right Sleeve from Shape Sleeve onward.

FINISHING

Weave in ends and block to measurements. For sizes 1, 2, 3 & 4 only, sew a button to left neck edge to correspond with buttonhole.

a. Finished chest (fullest point) circumference: 44 (47, 49, 52, 54, 58, 62, 65, 69)cm / 17½ (18¾, 19½, 20¾, 21½, 23¼, 24¾, 26, 27½)"
b. Body Length (hem to underarm): 12.5 (15, 16, 17.5, 19, 20.5, 23, 25.5, 28)cm / 5 (6, 6½, 7, 7½, 8, 9, 10, 11)"
c. Upper Sleeve Circumference: 19 (20, 22, 23, 24, 25, 26, 27, 28)cm / 7½ (8, 8¾, 9¼, 9½, 10, 10½, 10¾, 11¼)"
d. Sleeve Length: 14 (15, 16.5, 17.5, 19, 20.5, 23, 25.5, 28)cm / 5½ (6, 6½, 7, 7½, 8, 9, 10, 11)"
e. Yoke Depth (below neckband to underarm): 12 (12.5, 12.5, 13, 14, 14.5, 14.5, 15, 15.5)cm / 4¾ (5, 5, 5¼, 5½, 5¾, 5¾, 6, 6¼)"
f. Neck Opening: 30 (30, 32, 32, 34, 34, 36, 36, 36)cm / 12 (12, 12¾, 12¾, 13½, 13½, 14½, 14½, 14½)"

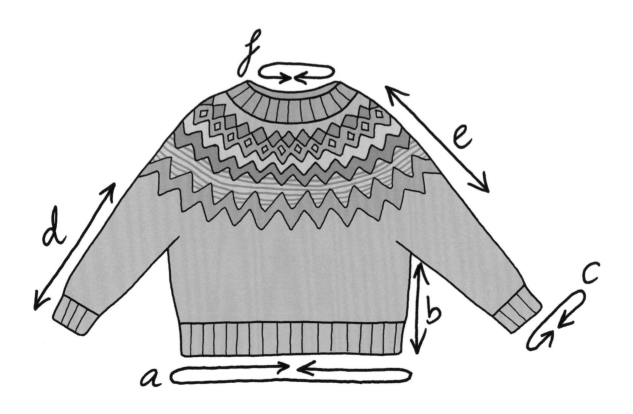

Sizes 1, 2 & 3 ONLY

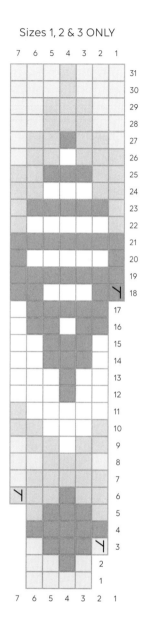

Sizes 4, 5, 6 & 7 ONLY

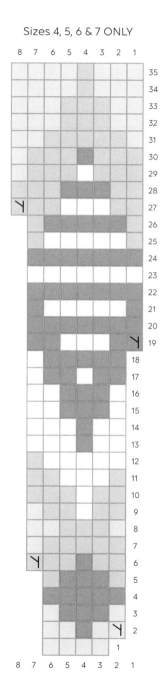

Sizes 8 & 9 ONLY

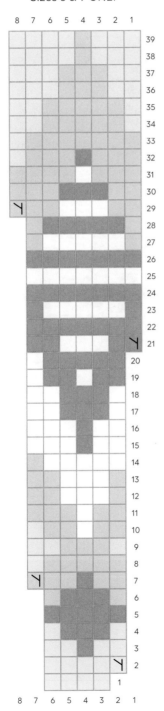

Key

	knit
Y	M1
	Yarn A
	Yarn B
	Yarn C
	Yarn D

Mini Norn

by Lydia Gluck

Norn's design lends itself extremely well to kids' growing bodies! Stretchy garter stitch and a generous neck opening means it can fit for more than just one season. There are also a myriad of ways to customise *Norn* to a child's sometimes very specific tastes: long sleeved, short sleeved, striped, solid, with a cable detail or without - there's a version of *Norn* for every kid.

Our grown-up version has served us well year after year since it was first published in our magazine way back in 2012, and we're sure the mini version will serve the little ones in your life for a very long time to come.

#MiniNorn

Sizes: 1 (2, 3, 4, 5, 6, 7, 8, 9)
To fit: 0-3 mths (3-6 mths, 6-12 mths, 12-18 mths, 1-2 yrs, 2-4 yrs, 4-6 yrs, 6-8 yrs, 8-10 yrs)
Finished chest (fullest point) circumference: 42 (44.5, 48, 50, 55.5, 60, 65.5, 70, 74.5)cm / 16½ (17½, 19, 19¾, 21¾, 23½, 25¾, 27½, 29¼)" - to be worn with 2-3cm / 1" positive ease

Short sleeve version:

Approximately 282 (298, 322, 335, 373, 403, 439, 470, 500)m / 310 (328, 354, 369, 410, 443, 483, 517, 550)yds of DK-weight yarn.

Long sleeve version:

Approximately 373 (395, 426, 445, 493, 533, 582, 622, 662)m / 410 (435, 469, 489, 542, 586, 640, 684, 728)yds of DK-weight yarn.

Sample 1 (Short-sleeve, stripe version, shown here and on pages 74, 81 and 83)
Lola (age 18 mths) is shown wearing a size 4.
The Uncommon Thread BFL Light DK (DK-weight; 100% superwash Blue Faced Leicester wool; 225m / 246yds per 100g skein)
Shades:
Yarn A: Golden Praline; 1 (1, 1, 1, 1, 1, 1, 2, 2) skeins
Yarn B: Sorbet; 1 (1, 1, 1, 1, 1, 1, 2, 2) skeins
Gauge: 18 sts & 32 rounds = 10cm / 4" over Garter st on 5.5mm needles, after blocking.
Needles: 5.5mm / US 9 needles circular needle, 40-80cm / 16-32" length (depending on size worked) AND needles suitable for working small circumferences in the round.
Note: Begin the yoke using needles suitable for working small circumferences in the round, then change to circular needles as the circumference increases.
Always use a needle size that will result in the correct gauge after blocking.
Notions: 10 stitch markers, tapestry needle, cable needle
Notes: *Norn* is knit in Garter st from the top down and in the round. We've shown two samples that are a mash up of the optional details adorning our grown-up version; with a short sleeve, stripe version omtting the cable detail (sample 1) or a long sleeve version in a solid colour with the cable detail (sample 2).
Adult version published in *Pom Pom Quarterly* Issue 3: Winter 2012.

Stitch Glossary

4/4 LC: Sl 4 to cable needle, hold at front, k4, k4 from cable needle.
4/4 RC: Sl 4 to cable needle, hold at back, k4, k4 from cable needle.

Mini Pom

Sample 2 (Long-sleeve, cable version, shown here)
Sabine (age 5 yrs) is shown wearing a size 7.

The Uncommon Thread BFL Light DK (DK-weight; 100% superwash Blue Faced Leicester wool; 225m / 246yds per 100g skein)
Shade: Seascape; 2 (2, 2, 2, 2, 3, 3, 3, 3) skeins

PATTERN BEGINS
YOKE
Using shorter circular needle, cast on 60 (66, 66, 72, 72, 75, 75, 80, 84) sts. Join to work in the round being careful not to twist sts. PM to indicate beg of round.

Round 1: [P6 (6, 6, 6, 6, 5, 5, 5, 6), PM] to end. *10 (11, 11, 12, 12, 15, 15, 16, 14) markers placed*
Round 2: Knit.
Round 3: Purl.
Inc round: *K to 1 st before marker, kfb, SM; rep from * to end. *10 (11, 11, 12, 12, 15, 15, 16, 14) sts inc*
Working in Garter st, rep Inc round every foll 4th round a further 4 (3, 4, 0, 2, 0, 0, 0, 2) times. *110 (110, 121, 84, 108, 90, 90, 96, 126) sts*
Rep Inc round every 6th round 2 (3, 3, 6, 5, 4, 2, 2, 4) times. *130 (143, 154, 156, 168, 150, 120, 128, 182) sts*

Sizes 6, 7, 8 & 9 ONLY:
Rep Inc round every 8th round 2 (4, 4, 2) times. *180 (180, 192, 210) sts*

ALL sizes again:
Next round: Purl, removing markers except for beg of round.
Next round: Knit, evenly increasing 6 (5, 0, 6, 4, 0, 6, 6, 0) sts across round. *136 (148, 154, 162, 172, 180, 186, 198, 210) sts*

Work even in Garter st if necessary until yoke measures 10.5 (11.5, 12.5, 13, 14, 14.5, 15.5, 15.5, 17)cm / 4¼ (4½, 5, 5, 5½, 5¾, 6, 6, 6¾)" from cast-on edge, ending with a purl round.

Divide Body and Sleeves
Next round: [K36 (38, 39, 41, 44, 48, 51, 55, 59), place next 32 (36, 38, 40, 42, 42, 42, 44, 46) sts on hold for sleeve, using the backwards-loop method cast on 2 (2, 4, 4, 6, 6, 8, 8, 8) sts for underarm] twice. *76 (80, 86, 90, 100, 108, 118, 126, 134) sts*

BODY
Set-up round: P3 (3, 2, 2, 1, 1, 0, 0, 0), PM for new beg of round, p30 (32, 35, 37, 42, 46, 51, 55, 59), PM, k8, PM, p30 (32, 35, 37, 42, 46, 51, 55, 59), PM, k8.

Round 1: Knit.
Round 2: [P to marker, k8] twice.
Rounds 3-8: Rep rounds 1-2 three times.
Round 9: K to marker, 4/4 LC, k to marker, 4/4 RC.
Round 10: [P to marker, k8] twice.
Rep rounds 1-10 a further 2 (2, 3, 3, 3, 4, 4, 5, 6) times.

Sizes 1, 5 & 6 ONLY: Knit 1 round.
Sizes 2, 3, 7, 8, & 9 ONLY: *K to marker decreasing 2 (1, 1, 1, 1) sts evenly, SM, k8; rep from * once more. *76 (84, 116, 124, 132) sts*
Size 4 ONLY: *K to marker increasing 1 st evenly, SM, k8; rep from * once more. *92 sts*

ALL sizes again
Ribbing
Round 1: [P2, k2] to 2 sts before marker, p2, k8, [p2, k2] to 2 sts before marker, p2, k8.
Rounds 2-7: Rep round 1.
Round 8: [P2, k2] to 2 sts before marker, p2, 4/4 LC, [p2, k2] to 2 sts before marker, p2, 4/4 RC.
Rounds 9-10: Rep round 1.
Cast off loosely in patt.

SLEEVES (both alike)
Using needles suitable for working small circumferences in the round, with RS facing and beg at RH end of underarm, pick up and knit 1 st in gap between underarm cast-on edge and sleeve sts, pick up and knit 2 (2, 4, 4, 6, 6, 8, 8, 8) sts from cast-on, pick up and knit 1 st in gap between underarm cast-on edge and sleeve sts, k across 32 (36, 38, 40, 42, 42, 42, 44, 46) held sleeve sts to last 2 (2, 1, 1, 0, 0, 0, 0, 0) sts, PM for new beg of rnd. *36 (40, 44, 46, 50, 50, 52, 54, 56) sts*
Sizes 7, 8 & 9 ONLY: Remove marker, k1, PM for new beg of round.
ALL sizes again: K8, p to end.

Version A: Short Sleeves
Sizes 1, 2, 3, 7 & 9 ONLY:
Next round (dec): K8, ssk, k to last 2 sts, k2tog, k2. *34 (38, 42, 50, 54) sts*

Sizes 4, 5, 6 & 8 ONLY: Knit 1 round.

ALL sizes again:
Round 1: K8, p to end. *34 (38, 42, 46, 50, 50, 50, 54, 54) sts*
Round 2: Knit.
Rounds 3-6: Rep rounds 1-2.
Round 7: Rep round 1.
Round 8:
First Sleeve only: 4/4 LC, k to end.
Second Sleeve only: 4/4 RC, k to end.
Rounds 9-10: Rep rounds 1-2.
Proceed to Ribbing.

Version B: Long Sleeves
Note: Cable repeat and decreases are worked **AT THE SAME TIME**. Read ahead to the end of this section before continuing.

Round 1: Knit.
Round 2: K8, p to end.
Rounds 3-8: Rep rounds 1-2.
Round 9:
First Sleeve ONLY: 4/4 LC, k to end.
Second Sleeve ONLY: 4/4 RC, k to end.
Round 10: K8, p to end.
Rep these 10 rounds an additional 2 (3, 3, 4, 4, 4, 5, 5, 6) times, then work rounds 1-6 once more.

AT THE SAME TIME, work Dec round on round 2 of sleeve and then every 6 (6, 4, 6, 4, 4, 6, 6, 6)th round a further 4 (6, 8, 7, 9, 9, 8, 9, 10) times as follows:
Dec round: K8, ssk, patt to last 2 sts, k2tog. *2 sts dec*

After decreases are complete, there will be 26 (26, 26, 30, 30, 30, 34, 34, 34) sts.

Work even after last dec round if necessary until Sleeve measures 10.5 (14, 14, 17, 17, 17, 20, 20, 23)cm / 4¼ (5½, 5½, 6¾, 6¾, 6¾, 7¾, 7¾, 9)" or 5cm / 2" less than desired length, ending on round 6 of cable pattern.

ALL sizes again:
Round 1: K8, p to end.
Round 2:
First Sleeve ONLY: 4/4 LC, k to end.
Second Sleeve ONLY: 4/4 RC, k to end.
Round 3: K8, p to end.
Round 4: Knit.
Proceed to Ribbing.

BOTH Versions:
Ribbing
Round 1: K8, p2, [k2, p2] to end.
Rounds 2-7: Rep round 1.
Round 8:

First Sleeve ONLY: 4/4 LC, p2, [k2, p2] to end.
Second Sleeve ONLY: 4/4 RC, p2, [k2, p2] to end.
Rounds 9-12: Rep round 1.
Cast off loosely in patt.

FINISHING
Weave in ends and wet block to measurements.

a. Chest (fullest point) circumference: 42 (44.5, 48, 50, 55.5, 60, 65.5, 70, 74.5)cm / 17 (17¾, 19, 20, 22¼, 24, 26¼, 28, 29¾)"
b. Body length (underarm to hem): 12.5 (12.5, 15.5, 15.5, 15.5, 19, 19, 22, 25)cm / 5 (5, 6¼, 6¼, 6¼, 7½, 7½, 8¾, 10)"
c. Yoke depth: 9.5 (10, 11.5, 12, 12.5, 13.5, 14.5, 15, 16.5)cm / 3¾ (4, 4½, 4¾, 5, 5¼, 5¾, 6, 6½)"
d. Sleeve length (Version A: Short Sleeve): 7.5cm / 3"
e. Sleeve length (Version B: Long Sleeve): 15.5 (19, 19, 22, 22, 22, 25, 25, 28)cm / 6¼ (7½, 7½, 8¾, 8¾, 8¾, 10, 10, 11¼)"
f. Upper arm circumference: 20 (22, 24.5, 25.5, 27.5, 27.5, 29, 30, 31)cm / 8 (8¾, 9¾, 10¼, 11, 11, 11½, 12, 12½)"
g. Cuff circumference (Version B: Long Sleeve): 14.5 (14.5, 14.5, 16.5, 16.5, 16.5, 19, 19, 19)cm / 5¾ (5¾, 5¾, 6¾, 6¾, 6¾, 7½, 7½, 7½)"

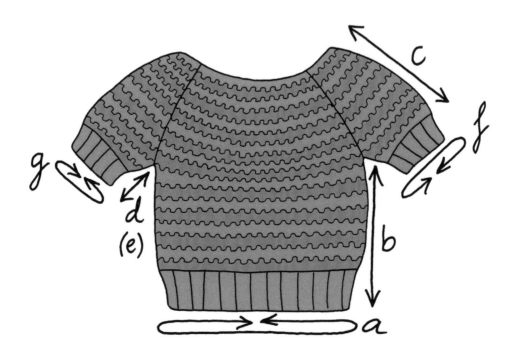

Mini Pom

Mini Pom Scarf

by Meghan Fernandes

By far the easiest and cosiest way to keep kids warm when out and about is a keyhole scarf! This scarf conceals a secret, hidden slot through which you can pull one pom pom to ensure it stays snug and never slips off. The pom poms are a fun and squishy touch that, for kids, are as entertaining as they are cute to wear. And the best part? Even very little children can help you wind the yarn to make the pom poms, meaning they get to help out their favourite grown-ups - something we know they love to do!

#MiniPomScarf

Sample 1 (checked version, shown here and on pages 84, 88, 89 and 92)
Lola (age 18 mths) is shown wearing a size 2.
Qing Fibre Dashing DK (DK-weight, 100% Merino wool; 225m / 246yds per 100g skein)
Shades:
Yarn A: Acid Apple; 1 skein
Yarn B: Ayre; 1 skein
Gauge: 22 sts & 26 rows = 10cm / 4" over St st pattern on 4mm needles after blocking.
Needles: 4mm / US 6 straight or circular needle
Always use a needle/hook size that will result in the correct gauge after blocking.
Notions: 8.5cm / 3⅜" pom pom maker, tapestry needle
Notes: This type of scarf is known as a keyhole scarf, where one end can be pulled through the other to secure. The scarf is knit flat and then seamed to make a tube, leaving an opening at one end to pull one pom pom through and secure around the child's neck. Working the scarf flat rather than in the round ensures the fabric lays flat when seamed and finished, especially the colourwork version.

Sample 2 (purple version, shown here and on page 91)
Sample shown is size 2.
The Uncommon Thread Posh DK (DK-weight; 70% wool, 20% silk, 10% cashmere; 229m / 250yds per 115g skein)
Shade: Ripe Plum; 1 (1, 2) skeins

Sizes: 1 (2, 3)
To fit: Baby (Toddler, Child)
Finished length (excluding pom poms): 31.5 (34, 37)cm / 12½ (13½, 14½)"
Yarn: approximately 180 (215, 290) m / 197 (235, 317) yds of DK-weight yarn.

PATTERN BEGINS

Cast on 34 (42, 50) sts.

SINGLE COLOUR VERSION ONLY

Work in St st until piece measures 25.5 (28, 31)cm / 10 (11, 12¼)" ending with a WS row.

Divide for Keyhole

Row 1 (RS)(dec): K2tog, k15 (19, 23), place remaining 17 (21, 25) stitches on hold. *16 (20, 24) sts*
Row 2 (WS): Purl.
Work in St st beginning with a knit row until piece measures 6cm / 2½" from divide, ending with a WS row.
Cast off all sts.

Place 17 (21, 25) held stitches back on needle and join yarn with RS facing.
Row 1 (RS)(dec): K15 (19, 23), k2tog. *16 (20, 24) sts*
Row 2 (WS): Purl.
Work in St st beginning with a knit row until piece measures 6cm / 2½" from divide, ending with a WS row.
Cast off all sts.

CHECKED VERSION ONLY

Commence Chart A, working rows 1-8 a total of 8 (9, 10) times.

Divide for Keyhole

Sizes 1 & 3 ONLY:

Next row (RS)(dec): K2tog (counts as first st of Chart B), work Chart B across first 16 (24) sts, place rem 17 (25) sts on hold. *16 (24) sts*
Work straight in patt from Chart B until rows 1-8 have been worked a total of 2 times.
Cast off all sts.

Place 17 (25) held sts back on needle and join yarn with RS facing.
Next row (RS)(dec): Work Chart B to last 2 sts, k2tog. *16 (24) sts*
Work straight in patt from Chart B until rows 1-8 have been worked a total of 2 times.
Cast off all sts.

Size 2 ONLY:

Next row (RS)(dec): K2tog (counts as first st of Chart C), work Chart C across first 20 sts, place rem 21 sts on hold. *20 sts*
Work straight in patt from Chart C until rows 1-8 have been worked a total of 2 times.
Cast off all sts.

Place 21 held sts back on needle and join yarn with RS facing.

Next row (RS)(dec): Work Chart C to last 2 sts, k2tog. *20 sts*
Work straight in patt from Chart C until rows 1-8 have been worked a total of 2 times.
Cast off all sts.

FINISHING
Wet block scarf and lay flat to dry. Then, using mattress stitch, seam long sides together from cast-on end up to the point where the keyhole split begins. Cut tail and weave in ends.

Make 2 pom poms using 8.5cm / 3⅜" pom pom maker.

Using a long length of yarn, work running stitch around the opening of the cast-on edge of the scarf. Pull yarn tightly to gather the edge together (akin to the top of a hat). Use the long tail to secure one pom pom to the end of the scarf.

Repeat for the cast-off end of the scarf, working one side and then the other of the keyhole split fabric, joining them together as you go before gathering. Use the long tail to secure the second pom pom to this end of the scarf. Weave in any remaining ends.

a. Finished length (excluding pom poms): 31.5 (34.5, 37.5)cm / 12½ (13½, 14¾)"
b. Finished width: 7.5 (9.5, 11.5)cm / 3 (3¾, 4½)"

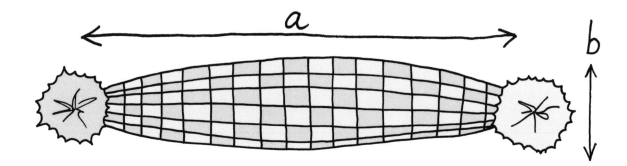

Chart A

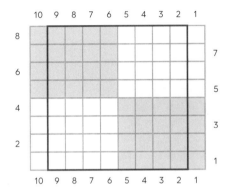

Chart B (Sizes 1 & 3 ONLY)

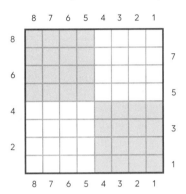

Chart C (Size 2 ONLY)

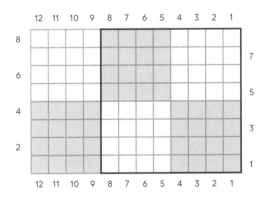

Key

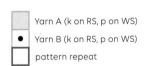

Yarn A (k on RS, p on WS)

● Yarn B (k on RS, p on WS)

pattern repeat

Mini Battenberg

by Gina Fama Röckenwagner

The most fanciful of desserts, the Battenberg cake, inspired this crochet cardigan that is as fun to wear as it is to make. Making piles of simple granny squares is always satisfying and the lucky little recipient can even help you stack and count them as you go. The wide sleeves and V-neck construction also mean this will be one that children can wear for multiple years - a real win for handmade garments!

#MiniBattenberg

Sizes: 1 (2, 3, 4, 5, 6, 7, 8, 9)
To fit: 0-3 mths (3-6 mths, 6-12 mths, 12-18 mths, 1-2 yrs, 2-4 yrs, 4-6 yrs, 6-8 yrs, 8-10 yrs)
Finished chest circumference: 47 (49.5, 56, 58.5, 63.5, 70, 72.5, 75, 77.5)cm / 18½ (19½, 22, 23, 25, 27½, 28½, 29½, 30½)" – to be worn with 5-10cm / 2-4" positive ease
Yarn A: approximately 220 (255, 290, 330, 380, 460, 540, 630, 680)m / 245 (280, 320, 360, 420, 505, 595, 690, 750)yds of sport-weight yarn
Yarn B: approximately 50 (50, 55, 55, 70, 75, 80, 85, 90)m / 55 (55, 60, 60, 75, 80, 85, 95, 100)yds of sport-weight yarn
Yarn C: approximately 50 (50, 55, 55, 70, 75, 80, 85, 90)m / 55 (55, 60, 60, 75, 80, 85, 95, 100)yds of sport-weight yarn
Yarn D: approximately 50 (50, 55, 55, 70, 75, 80, 85, 90)m / 55 (55, 60, 60, 75, 80, 85, 95, 100)yds of sport-weight yarn

Yarn E: approximately 50 (50, 55, 55, 70, 75, 80, 85, 90)m / 55 (55, 60, 60, 75, 80, 85, 95, 100)yds of sport-weight yarn
Yarn F: approximately 50 (50, 55, 55, 70, 75, 80, 85, 90)m / 55 (55, 60, 60, 75, 80, 85, 95, 100)yds of sport-weight yarn
Yarn G: approximately 50 (50, 55, 55, 70, 75, 80, 85, 90)m / 55 (55, 60, 60, 75, 80, 85, 95, 100)yds of sport-weight yarn
Sample (Multi, shown here)
Camila (age 3 yrs) is wearing a size 6.
BC Garn Summer in Kashmir (sportweight; 90% organic cotton, 10% cashmere; 165m / 180yds per 50g ball)
Shades:
Yarn A: 01 Natural; 3 skeins
Yarn B: 04 Dusty Pink; 1 skein
Yarn C: 28 Denim; 1 skein
Yarn D: 09 Brick Red; 1 skein
Yarn E: 23 Rainforest; 1 skein
Yarn F: 15 Bras;, 1 skein
Yarn G: 16 Kiwi; 1 skein
Gauge: One Square with 1 round of double crochet border = 7cm / 2¾" square using 2.75mm hook after blocking.
One Square without border = 5.5cm / 2¼" square square using 2.75mm hook
Needles: 2.75mm / US C crochet hook
2.25mm / US B crochet hook (for button band)
3.25mm / US D crochet hook (for joining)
Always use a hook size that will result in the correct gauge after blocking.
Notions: 7 locking stitch markers, 3 buttons 2.5cm / 1" diameter
Notes: *Battenberg* is constructed from a number of separately-worked granny squares. The squares are joined together while a double crochet border is worked; refer to the appropriate diagrams when laying out pieces and working the joining rows. Note that some sizes have half-squares at the side seams, and all sizes feature a triangle on each front; the remainder of the shapes are squares. Finally the garment pieces are joined and a button/buttonhole band worked around the front opening. If your squares are colourful and your border colour is light, adding a dash of white vinegar to your soaking basin will help prevent the colours from running. Alternatively, wash your squares separately before joining them.
Please see tutorial for help with the joining technique: *bit.ly/2X7hoXs*
Adult version published in *Pom Pom Quarterly* Issue 36: Spring 2021.

Stitch Glossary

Square (worked in the round)

Ch 4. Sl st in first ch to make a ring.

Round 1: Ch3 (counts as dc throughout), 2dc into ring, [ch3, 3dc into ring] 3 times, ch3, sl st in third of beg 3-ch to join. *Four 3-dc clusters*

Round 2: Ch3, 2dc in last ch sp of previous round, [(3dc, ch3, 3dc) into next 3-ch sp] 3 times, 3dc into next 3-ch sp (same sp as beg 2-dc), ch3, sl st in third of beg 3-ch to join. *Eight 3-dc clusters*

Round 3: Ch3, 2dc in last ch sp of previous round, [3dc into next sp between 3-dc clusters, (3dc, ch3, 3dc) into next 3-ch sp] 3 times, 3dc into next sp between 3-dc clusters, 3dc into next 3-ch sp (same sp as beg 2-dc), ch3, sl st in third of beg 3-ch to join. *Twelve 3-dc clusters*

Triangle (worked flat)

Ch 4. Sl st in first ch to make a ring.

Row 1 (RS): Ch3 (counts as dc throughout), 3dc into ring, ch3, 4dc into ring, turn. *Two 4-dc clusters*

Row 2 (WS): Ch3, 3dc into the sp directly below the 3-ch (between the first 2 dc of previous row), (3dc, ch3, 3dc) into next 3-ch sp, 4dc into the sp between the last 2 dc of previous row, turn. *Two 3-dc clusters, two 4-dc clusters*

Row 3 (RS): Ch3, 3dc into the sp directly below the 3-ch, 3dc into the sp between next two 3-dc clusters, (3dc, ch3, 3dc) into next 3-ch sp, 3dc into the sp between the next two 3-dc clusters, 4dc into the sp between the last 2 dc of previous row, turn. *Four 3-dc clusters, two 4-dc clusters*

Half Square (worked flat)

Ch4. Sl st in first ch to make a ring.

Row 1 (RS): Ch3 (counts as dc throughout), 2dc into ring, [ch3, 3dc into ring] twice, turn. *Three 3-dc clusters*

Row 2 (WS): Ch3, (3dc, ch3, 3dc) into first 3-ch sp, (3dc, ch3, 3dc) into next 3-ch sp, 1dc into the sp between the last 2 dc of previous row, turn. *Four 3-dc clusters*

Row 3 (RS): Ch3, 2dc into the sp directly below the 3-ch (between the first 2 dc of previous row), (3dc, ch3, 3dc) into next 3-ch sp, 3dc into the sp between next two 3-dc clusters, (3dc, ch3, 3dc) into next 3-ch sp, 3dc into the sp between the last 2 dc of previous row, turn. *Seven 3-dc clusters*

PATTERN BEGINS

Using 2.75mm hook, make a total of 17 (19, 28, 28, 38, 44, 44, 58, 58) Squares, 6 (6, 0, 0, 0, 16, 16, 16, 16) Half Squares, and 2 Triangles as foll:

Left Front

Make 2 (2, 5, 5, 5, 6, 6, 6, 6) Squares, 3 (3, 0, 0, 0, 4, 4, 4, 4) Half Squares, and 1 Triangle

Right Front

Make 2 (2, 5, 5, 5, 6, 6, 6, 6) Squares, 3 (3, 0, 0, 0, 4, 4, 4, 4) Half Squares, and 1 Triangle

Back

Make 9 (9, 12, 12, 12, 16, 16, 16, 16) Squares and 0 (0, 0, 0, 0, 8, 8, 8, 8) Half Squares

Sleeves

Make 2 (3, 3, 3, 8, 8, 8, 15, 15) Squares **for each sleeve**.

Join Squares

Lay out your pieces according to the diagram of the size you are making, with RS facing up.

Referring to the basic join diagram, using 3.25mm hook, join your pieces using yarn B as foll:

Join yarn B to top right-hand corner of the first square of your piece. The first square is the square at the top right corner.

Top side and left-hand side of Square 1: Ch3, 2dc in the 3-ch sp directly below, 1dc into each of next 9 dc, (3dc, ch3, 3dc) into the 3-ch sp, 1dc into each of next 9 dc, 3dc into the 3-ch sp, ch1.

Right-hand side of Square 2: 1dc into the bottom right-hand corner of the next square (the next square is directly to the left of the first square), remove the loop from the hook and insert the hook from right to left into the top of the last dc worked into the bottom left corner of the previous square, pulling the loop through. [Dc again into the 3-ch sp of the new square, remove the stitch from the hook, thread the hook from right to left into the top of the corresponding stitch on the previous square] twice. Continue to work dc up the right-hand side of the second square as set, threading the stitch through the border on the first square after every stitch. At the corner, 3dc into the 3-ch sp, continuing to join to the left hand border of the first square as you go, ch3.

Top side of Square 2: 3dc into the 3-ch sp, 1dc into each of next 9 dc, 3dc into next 3-ch sp, ch 3.

Left side of Square 2: 3dc into the 3-ch sp, 1dc into each of next 9 dc, 3dc into next 3-ch sp, ch1.

Continue to join squares in this manner until all the squares from the first row are joined. Now work across bottom edge of row as foll:

Bottom edge of the first row of squares: [3dc into the 3-ch sp, 1dc into each of next 9 dc, 3dc into next 3-ch sp, ch2, sl st into the join between squares, ch2] to end, ending the final repeat with ch1.

Continue to join squares as set, joining the top edges to the bottom edge of the previous row as you work the border. After working the bottom edge of the last row of squares, work up the right-hand side of the piece to complete the border of the garment piece.

Join all of the squares/other shapes together in this way until you have assembled two front pieces, two sleeve pieces, and the back piece. **Note:** Refer to the upper front join diagram when working the fronts as they include some irregular shapes.

SPACER ROWS

Body

With yarn B, double crochet 2 (3, 0, 1, 3, 0, 1, 2, 3) rows along the outside edge of both front pieces and the back piece.

Sleeves

With yarn B, double crochet 1 (2, 3, 4, 0, 2, 4, 1, 2) rows along one long edge of both sleeves (this will be the cuff edge).

Join Sleeves

Aligning the squares, join the shoulder seams using single crochet. Join the sleeves to the body using single crochet, taking care to match the centre line of the sleeve to the shoulder seam. Join the underarm seams and the side seams.

Neckline and button band

With RS facing, using 2.25mm hook, join yarn B to bottom corner of right front.
Row 1 (RS): Ch1, 1sc into every dc and ch around the front opening and neckline to bottom corner of left front, turn.
Row 2 (WS): Rep row 1.
Mark placement for 3 evenly-spaced buttonholes along the right front opening edge using stitch markers or waste yarn.

Row 3 (RS): Ch3, 1dc into each sc to end, at the same time working buttonhole at each marked point as foll: ch1, skip 1 st, 1dc into next st (buttonhole made). Turn.
Rows 4-5: Rep row 1.
Fasten off.

FINISHING

Weave in ends and block. Sew on buttons opposite the buttonholes.

a. Chest (fullest point) circumference: 47 (49.5, 56, 58.5, 63.5, 70, 72.5, 75, 77.5)cm / 18½ (19½, 22, 23, 25, 27½, 28½, 29½, 30½)"
b. Length (back neck to hem): 21 (21, 21, 21, 21, 28, 28, 35, 35) cm / 8¼ (8¼, 8¼, 8¼, 8¼, 11, 11, 13¾, 13¾)"
c. Sleeve circumference: 14 (21, 21, 21, 28, 28, 28, 35, 35)cm / 5 ½ (8¼, 8¼, 8¼, 11, 11, 11, 13¾, 13¾)"
d. Drop shoulder width: 4.5 (5, 7, 7.5, 9, 10, 11, 11.5, 12)cm / 1¾ (2, 2¾, 3, 3½, 4, 4¼, 4½, 4¾)"
e. Sleeve piece length: 7 (8.5, 9, 9.5, 14, 15, 16.5, 21.5, 22)cm / 2¾ (3¼, 3½, 3¾, 5½, 6, 6½, 8½, 8¾)" (Note: This does not include the additional length provided by the drop shoulder.)
f. Back neck width: 12.7cm / 5.5"

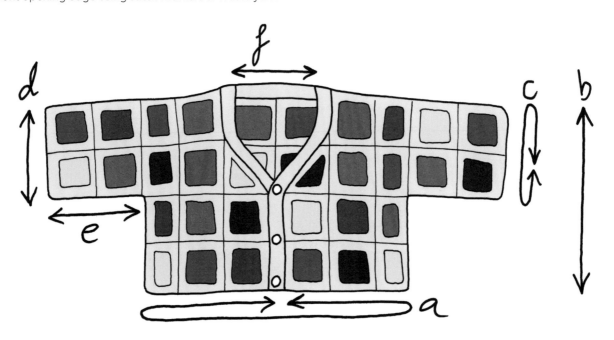

Layout Diagrams

Key

— spacer rows   --- shoulder line   ⟵ start here

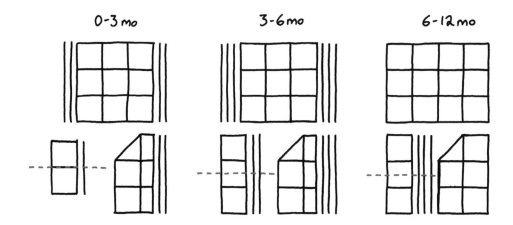

0-3 mo   3-6 mo   6-12 mo

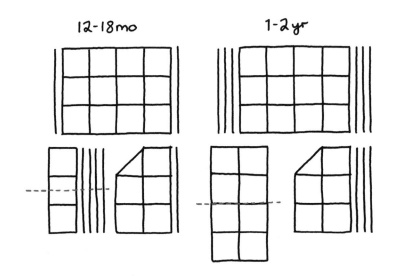

12-18mo   1-2 yr

Diagram for basic join:

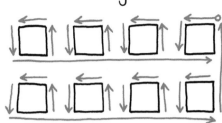

Diagram for joining upper front squares:

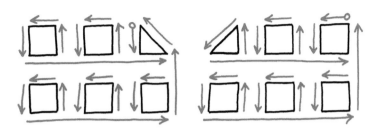

2-4 yr

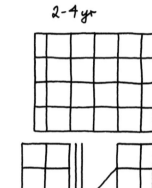

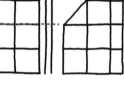

4-6 yr

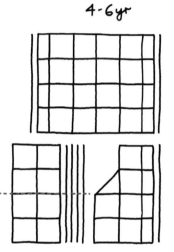

6-8 yr

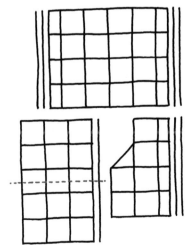

8-10 yr

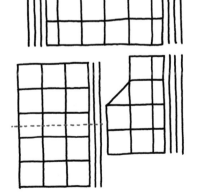

Mini Pom

Mini Skipworth

by Meghan Fernandes

The original *Skipworth* mitts were published in the very first issue of our magazine, *Pom Pom Quarterly* and they've been a staple in our winter wardrobes ever since. Simple and squishy, we think kiddos will especially love the texture of the soft garter stitch ridges on their hands as they keep warm in cold temps. The grown-up *Skipworths* are fingerless mitts, but we thought tiny hands could use a bit of extra warmth!

As an added bonus, there's the option of an i-cord string to attach them, meaning the likelihood of losing one (or both!) is reduced dramatically. We like to tuck the strings into the sleeves and backs of our littles' jackets so they stay put.

#MiniSkipworth

Pattern: Mini Skipworth - Keeping Little Mitts Toasty and Together

Needles: 3.5mm / US 4 **AND** 4mm / US 6 knitting needles suitable for working small circumferences in the round.
4 mm / US 6 double pointed needles for I-cord (optional)
Always use a needle size that will result in the correct gauge after blocking.

Notions: 3 stitch markers, tapestry needle

Notes: Please note there is no thumb for Size 1 (0-12 mths).
Mini Skipworth mitts are worked in the round in garter stitch, from the cuff upwards. Size 1 (0-12 mths) has no thumb, while the remaining sizes work increasess to create the thumb gusset. Optional mitten cord is sewn to the completed mitts.

Adult version published in *Pom Pom Quarterly* Issue 1: Summer 2012.

Sizes: 1 (2, 3, 4, 5, 6)
To fit: 0-12 mths (1-2 yrs, 2-4 yrs, 4-6 yrs, 6-8 yrs, 8-10 yrs)
Finished hand circumference: 11 (12.5, 13.5, 15, 16.5, 17.5)cm / 4½ (5, 5½, 6, 6½, 7)"
Yarn: approximately 55 (66, 78, 111, 133, 163)m / 64 (73, 86, 122, 145, 178)yds of DK-weight yarn.
Sample (Blue, shown here)
Lola (age 18 mths) is shown wearing a size 3.
John Arbon Textiles Knit by Numbers DK (DK weight; 100% merino wool; 250m / 273yds per 100g skein)
Shade: KBN97; 1 skein
Gauge: 20 sts & 44 rows = 10 cm / 4" over garter stitch in the round on 4mm needles after blocking

Pattern: Mini Skipworth - Keeping Little Mitts Toasty and Together

PATTERN BEGINS (both alike)
Cuff
Using smaller needles, and a loose/stretchy method, cast on 23 (25, 27, 31, 33, 35) sts. Divide sts evenly between needles, join for working in the round being careful not to twist. PM to indicate beg of round.

Round 1: Purl.

Round 2: Knit.

Rounds 1-2 set Garter Stitch in the round.

Rep rounds 1-2 a further 4 (5, 6, 7, 8, 9) times, then work round 1 once more. *6 (7, 8, 9, 10, 11) garter ridges*

Change to larger needles.

Note: There is no thumb gusset for Size 1. Place a marker into work to indicate end of cuff. Skip to "All Sizes again".

SIZES 2-6 ONLY (there is no thumb for Size 1):
Thumb Gusset
Round 1: K1, M1L, PM, k to last st, PM, M1R, k1. - *(27, 29, 33, 35, 37) sts*

Round 2: P to end.

Round 3: K to marker, M1L, SM, knit to second marker, SM, M1R, k to end. *2 sts inc*

Round 4: P to end.

Round 5: K to end.

Round 6: P to end.

Repeat rounds 3-6 a further - (0, 1, 1, 2, 3) times. - *(29, 33, 37, 41, 45) sts total; - (8, 10, 12, 14, 16) sts between thumb gusset markers*

Work in garter st until piece measures - (2.5, 3, 3.5, 3.5, 4.5) cm / - (1, 1¼, 1½, 1½, 1¾)" from beginning of thumb increases, ending with a knit round.

Next round: Removing markers as you come to them, purl to last - (4, 5, 6, 7, 8) sts, place remaining sts AND following - (4, 5, 6, 7, 8) sts from beginning of round on hold for thumb. Rejoin for working in the round and PM to indicate new beginning of round. - *(8, 10, 12, 14, 16) sts on hold for thumb, - (21, 23, 25, 27, 29) sts for hand*

ALL sizes again
Continue working in garter st in the round until piece measures 9 (9.5, 10, 12, 13.5, 15)cm / 3½ (3¾, 4, 4¾, 5¼, 6)" from base of thumb gusset / marker at top of cuff, ending with a purl round.

Decrease for top of hand:
Round 1 (dec): [K3, k2tog] to last 3 (1, 3, 0, 2, 4) sts, k to end. *19 (17, 19, 20, 22, 24) sts*

Round 2: P to end.

Round 3 (dec): [K2, k2tog] to last 3 (1, 3, 0, 2, 4) sts, k to end. *15 (13, 15, 15, 17, 19) sts*

Round 4: P to end.

Round 5 (dec): [K1, k2tog] to last 0 (1, 0, 0, 2, 1) sts, k to end. *10 (9, 10, 10, 12, 13) sts*

Round 6: P to end.

Round 7 (dec): K2tog to last 0 (1, 0, 0, 0, 1) st, k to end. *5 (5, 5, 6, 7, 7) sts*

Round 8: Purl.

Cut yarn, leaving a long tail. Thread tail on tapestry needle and draw through remaining stitches to close.

Sizes 2-6 ONLY:
Thumb
Place - (8, 10, 12, 14, 16) held thumb sts back onto needles, dividing evenly.

Rejoin yarn where thumb meets hand.

Purl first - (4, 5, 6, 7, 8) sts. PM to mark new beg of round. - *(8, 10, 12, 14, 16) sts*

Work in garter st in the round for - (1.25, 2, 2.5, 3, 3)cm / - (½, ¾, 1, 1¼, 1¼)", ending with a purl round.

Decrease for top of thumb:
Round 1: K2tog around. - *(4, 5, 6, 7, 8) sts*

Round 2: Purl.

Cut yarn. Thread tail on tapestry needle and draw through remaining stitches to close.

FINISHING
Sew gap closed where thumb meets hand. Weave in remaining ends and block to measurements.

Mitten Cord (optional)
Using larger double pointed needles, cast on 4 sts, leaving a long tail.

Step 1: Slide sts to opposite end of needle.

Step 2: Bring the working yarn across the back, knit 4 sts.

Repeat Steps 1-2 until your cord measures 59 (65.25, 78, 84.5, 91, 97)cm / 23¼ (25¾, 30¾, 33¼, 35¾, 38¼)".

Break yarn, leaving a long tail. Thread tail on tapestry needle and draw through remaining stitches to close.

Pattern: Mini Skipworth - Keeping Little Mitts Toasty and Together

Using the long tail at one end of the cord, sew the cord securely to the edge of the cuff of one mitten, on the thumb side. Repeat for the other end of the cord and the other mitten. Weave in ends.

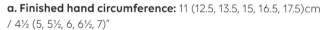

a. Finished hand circumference: 11 (12.5, 13.5, 15, 16.5, 17.5)cm / 4½ (5, 5½, 6, 6½, 7)"
b. Length: 10.5 (10.5, 11, 13, 15, 17)cm / 4¼ (4¼, 4½, 5¼, 6, 6¾)"

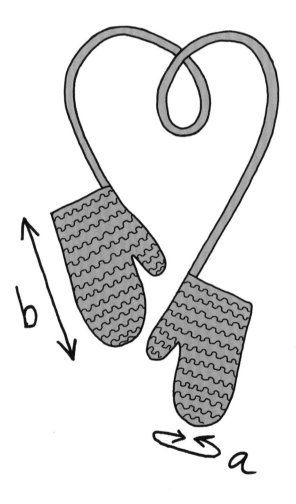

Mini Pom

Truffle

by Sophie Heathscott

Did you know that pigs were a popular lucky charm
in the late 19th and early 20th centuries in parts of
Europe? Sayings such as 'a pig in clover' are a nod to pigs
representing happiness and good luck. Fortuitous or not,
this piggy certainly makes a charming companion with its
adorable cuddly shape perfect for snuggling. Nifty shaping
techniques make for a virtually seamless and speedy knit -
you might end up making one for yourself too!

#MiniTrufflePig

Pattern: Truffle - The Perfect Piggy for Soft Snuggles

Notes: The pig starts at the centre of the snout using a pinhole cast-on (see page 119 for tutorial), and then increases out to form a circle. This is cast off, and stitches are picked up around the edge of the cast off piece to start the nose/face. The increases for the face are then worked in the round, safety eyes are inserted (if using) and then the body is worked. Decreases shape the bum, and then the tail is made by working an I-cord and stitching into place. The two ears are made separately, worked flat and sewn into place.

Finally, 4 legs are worked in the round and then sewn on. Safety eyes are used in the sample, make sure you are using an eye that has a retaining back that locks on to the fabric preventing the eyes from being pulled out.

If you are giving the toy to very small babies or children, you may want to embroider eyes instead.

A great alternative to stuffing is using wool scraps or old swatches, but please note that very bright colours may show through, depending what yarn you are using as a main colour.

One size: 25cm / 10" long x 14cm / 5¾" tall

Yarn: Approximately 120m / 130yds of worsted-weight yarn.

Sample (Pink, shown here)

Malabrigo Rios (worsted-weight; 100% superwash Merino wool; 192m / 210yds per 100g skein)

Shade: Melon (#707); 1 skein

Gauge: 20 sts & 28 rounds = 10 cm / 4" over St st on 4mm needles before blocking

Note that exact gauge is not essential for toys, but you should ensure a firm fabric so stuffing cannot escape

Needles: 4mm / US 6 needles, suitable for working small circumferences in the round.

Always use a needle size that will result in the correct gauge after blocking.

Notions: Stitch marker, safety eyes (10mm) or scrap yarn, stuffing, tapestry needle

Mini Pom

PATTERN BEGINS

Snout

Note: The finished pig will have the purl side of snout as the right side, however It is worked with the knit side facing for ease of knitting.

Using the pinhole method, cast on 5 sts.
Join to work in the round, being careful not to twist sts.
PM to indicate beginning of round.

Round 1: Knit.
Round 2: [K1, M1L] to end. *10 sts*
Rounds 3-4: Knit.
Round 5: [K1, M1L] to end. *20 sts*
Knit 4 rounds.

Cast off tightly (you can alter your tension or use a smaller needle) so that the fabric curls in after casting off. Thread a needle onto the cast-off tail and weave the gap closed between the first cast-off stitch and the last, making the cast-off a seamless circle. Weave in the end on the knit side (no need to trim, it will be hidden inside the toy). Make sure the cast-on tail is threaded through to the knit side of the work.

Turn the snout so the purl side is facing, it should look like a dome. With the cast-on edge facing you, pick up a stitch by inserting your right-hand needle tip into the top bump of stitch in the row above the cast-off. Skip the next bump, pick up a stitch in the next bump. Continue in this manner until you have picked up a total of 10 stitches. Join for working in the round, purl side facing out. PM to indicate beginning of round. *10 sts*

Round 1: Join yarn and knit.
Round 2: [K1, M1L] to end. *20 sts*
Knit 2 rounds.
Pause to weave in and secure the tail end for the yarn just joined.

Shaping Snout and Face
Round 1: K6, M1R, k8, M1L, k6. *22 sts*
Rounds 2, 4, 6, 8, 10, 12, 14, 16, 18: Knit.
Round 3: K7, M1R, k3, M1R, k2, M1L, k3, M1L, k7. *26 sts*
Round 5: K7, M1R, k4, M1R, k4, M1L, k4, M1L, k7. *30 sts*

Round 7: K7, M1R, k5, M1R, k6, M1L, k5, M1L, k7. *34 sts*
Round 9: K7, M1R, k6, M1R, k8, M1L, k6, M1L, k7. *38 sts*
Round 11: K2, M1L, k5, M1R, k7, M1R, k10, M1L, k7, M1L, k5, M1R, k2. *44 sts*
Round 13: K3, M1L, k5, M1R, k8, M1R, k12, M1L, k8, M1L, k5, M1R, k3. *50 sts*
Round 15: K4, M1L, k5, M1R, k9, M1R, k14, M1L, k9, M1L, k5, M1R, k4. *56 sts*
Round 17: K5, M1L, k15, M1R, k16, M1L, k15, M1R, k5. *60 sts*
Round 19: K6, M1L, k15, M1R, k18, M1L, k15, M1R, k6. *64 sts*

Stuff the face, paying attention to the snout to get a shape you find pleasing.

Note: If you are using safety eyes, insert these now before starting the body. Play around with positioning, eyes really make the character of a toy! The BOR marker is the bottom of the chin, use the increases on the face as a guide to make sure the eyes are balanced.

Knit straight for 36 rounds or 12cm / 4¾". Work measures approximately 20cm / 8" from snout.
Stuff the body, leaving a small gap at the top.

Bum Shaping
Note: While working the shaping, continue to fill the toy with stuffing. Make sure to leave a small gap at the top so you have space to maneuver your stitches and needles.

Set-up Round: [K2tog, k6, PM] to end. *56 sts*
Next Round: Knit, slipping markers as you come to them.
Round 1: [K2tog, knit to marker, SM] to end. *8 sts dec*
Round 2: Knit, slipping markers as you come to them.
Rep last 2 rounds until 8 sts remain.
Ensure body is fully stuffed to your liking before starting the final decrease. A chopstick is very handy for this stage of stuffing!
Next round: [K2tog] to end, removing markers. *4 sts*

Tail
Work i-cord across these 4 sts for 8cm / 3".
Cut yarn leaving 20cm / 8" tail, thread yarn tail onto tapestry needle, thread through stitches and pull tight, do not cut end.

Tail Finishing

Pass tapestry needle through end of the i-cord into the centre of the tube and bring out of the fabric about halfway along the length. Curl i-cord around into a 'p' shape, and secure in place by stitching through the base of the cord and catching the underneath of the i-cord to hold the curl in place. Secure the length of yarn you've used for sewing and bury the end in the stuffing in the body. These instructions for the tail are a guide only! Make your tail longer, make more loops, tie a knot or sew in place how you want!

Right Ear

Using the long-tail method, cast on 3 stitches.
Row 1 (WS): Sl1 pwise wyif, p2.
Row 2 (RS): Sl1 kwise wyib, k2.
Rows 3, 5, 7, 9, 11, 13, 15, 17, 19: Sl1 pwise wyif, p to end.
Row 4: Sl1 kwise wyib, M1R, k2. *4 sts*
Row 6: Sl1 kwise wyib, M1R, k3. *5 sts*
Row 8: Sl1 kwise wyib, M1R, k3, M1L, k1. *7 sts*
Row 10: Sl1 kwise wyib, M1R, k5, M1L, k1. *9 sts*
Row 12: Sl1 kwise wyib, M1R, k7, M1L, k1. *11 sts*
Row 14: Sl1 kwise wyib, M1R, k9, M1L, k1. *13 sts*
Row 16: Sl1 kwise wyib, M1R, k11, M1L, k1. *15 sts*
Row 18: Sl1 kwise wyib, M1R, k4, k2tog, ssk, k5, M1L, k1. *15 sts*
Row 20: Sl1 kwise wyib, k4, k2tog, ssk, k6. *13 sts*
Row 21: Sl1 pwise wyif, p4, p3tog, p5. *11 sts*
Row 22: Cast off, leaving a tail of at least 20cm / 8" for sewing.

Left Ear

Using the long-tail method, cast on 3 stitches.
Row 1 (WS): Sl1 pwise wyif, p2.
Row 2 (RS): Sl1 kwise wyib, k2.
Row 3, 5, 7, 9, 11, 13, 15, 17, 19: Sl1 pwise wyif, p to end.
Row 4: Sl1 kwise wyib, k1, M1L, k1. *4 sts*
Row 6: Sl1 kwise wyib, k2, M1L, k1. *5 sts*
Rows 8–22: Work as for right ear.
Note: You may want to place a locking stitch marker in the fabric of this ear to remind you it has the left ear shaping.

Pattern: Truffle - The Perfect Piggy for Soft Snuggles

Ear Finishing

Weave in the end at the tip of the ear. Wet block or steam ears to set the shape, letting the top of the ear curl over slightly. With snout towards you, pin ears either side of the head with WS facing, (remember one goes on the left!) and position them just after the last increase at the top of the head. Using cast off tail, sew ears securely onto the body.

Legs (make 4)

Using the long-tail method, cast on 20 sts, leaving a tail of at least 20cm / 8" for sewing.
Join to work in the round, being careful not to twist sts. PM to indicate beginning of round.

Rounds 1-10 : Knit.
Round 11: [K2tog] to end. *10 sts*
Round 12: [K2tog] to end. *5 sts*
Cut yarn, thread tail end onto a tapestry needle and thread through stitches, pull tightly and fasten off. Thread tail end through to wrong side and weave in, no need to cut as it will be hidden inside the leg.

Stuff legs and sew in place on body using the long cast-on tail.

Pinhole Cast-On

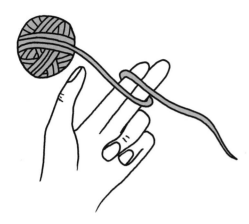

1. Wrap the yarn tail over two fingers as shown to create a loop.

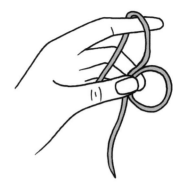

2. Slide the loop off your fingers, pinching the loop with your left hand so the yarn stays in this position.

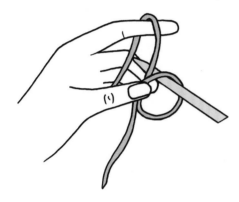

3. Insert needle tip through the loop and wrap the working yarn round the needle as if working a knit stitch.

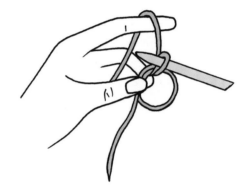

4. Draw the yarn through the loop, the yarn now sits on the needle as a stitch.

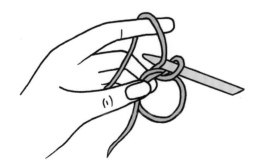

5. Work a yarn over.

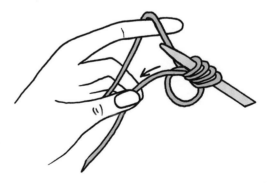

6. Repeat steps 3-5 for required number of stitches for cast-on. To finish, pull cast-on tail gently to close the loop, keeping it slightly loose. This can be tightened and adjusted after working first row of pattern to draw the stitches to a neat 'pinhole'.

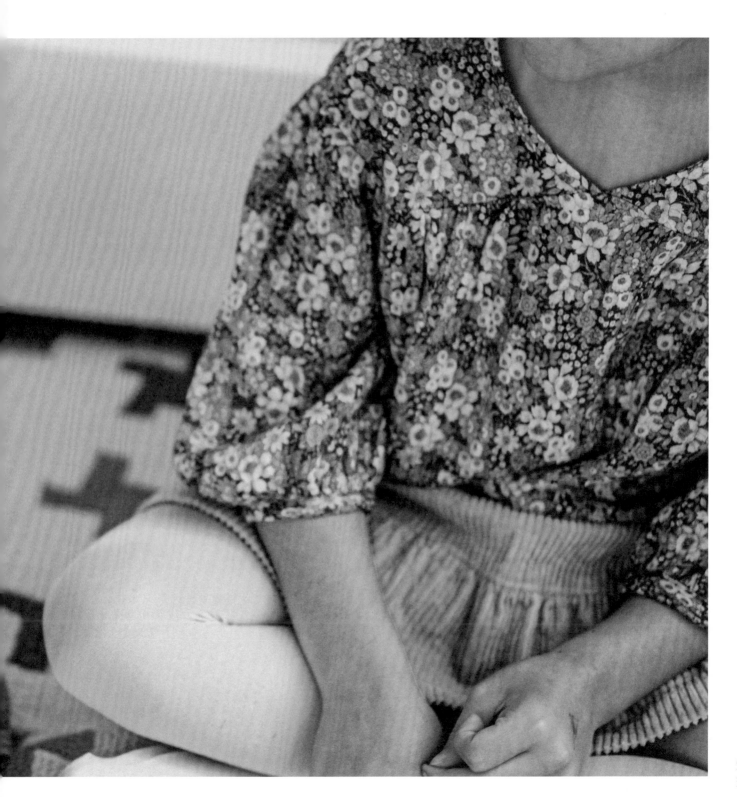

Colouring
Pages

Download and print the following
pages for lots of colour exploration!

Please see the download code
printed on the inside of the back cover.

Mini Pom

Colouring Pages

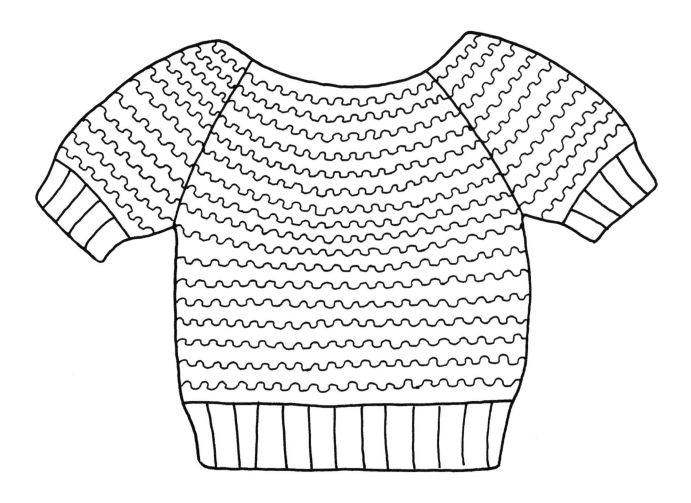

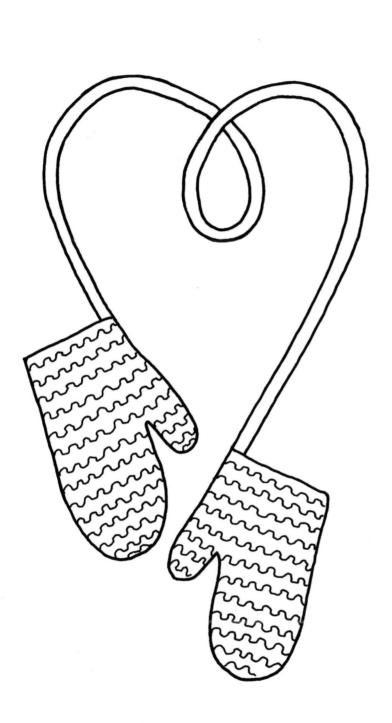
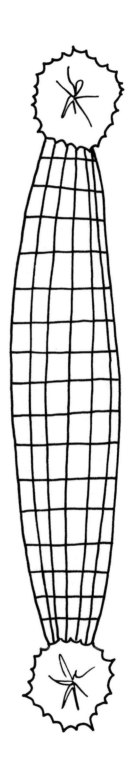

Colouring Pages

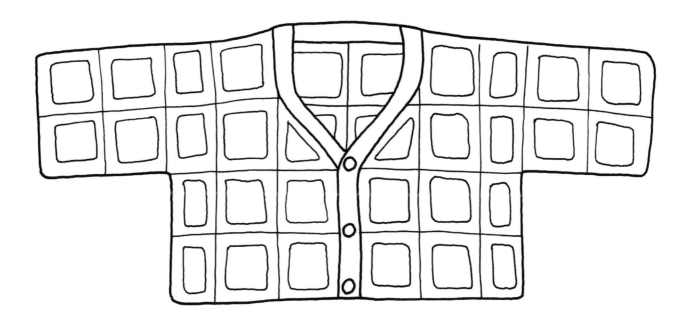

Colouring Pages

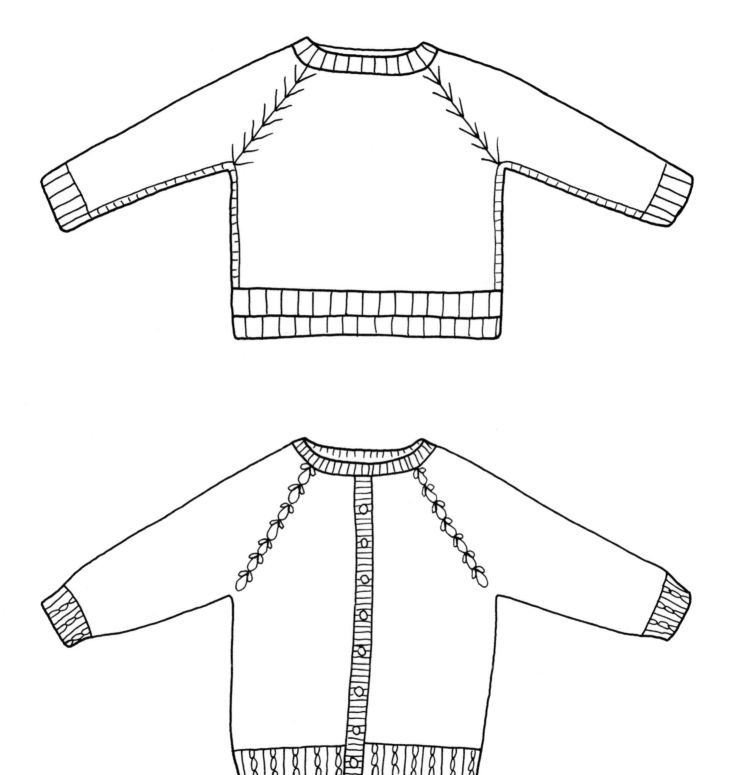

Contributors

Meghan Fernandes (she/her) is a knitting designer and instructor, as well as co-founder and editor of Pom Pom. After 10 years in London, she is now based in Austin, Texas, where she lives with her husband and young daughters. She revels in the challenge of making and enjoying knitwear for a hot climate. *@meghanaf*

Lydia Gluck (she/her) has always had a crafty streak, dabbling in everything from woodwork to papier mâché. Alongside her work at Pom Pom, Lydia is currently studying for an MA in Fine Art! When she's not making publications or art things she can be found horse riding, singing, or wild swimming. *@lydia_shmidia*

Alice Sleight (she/her) has been a maker all her life. She has dabbled in dressmaking, painting and even bookbinding but it is knitting that has stolen her heart. With a keen eye for detail and a love of solving problems, she adores pattern writing and turning knitwear dreams into a reality. *@alicesleight*

Chaitanya Muralidhara (she/her) is a tech editor and fibre enthusiast based in Boston, MA. She is passionate about patterns that empower crafters to create a handmade wardrobe. *@beginswithac*

Fiona Alice (she/her) is a knitwear designer, originally from Nova Scotia, Canada who now calls Helsinki, Finland home. In her spare time, Fiona enjoys exploring Helsinki by bike, gardening at her local park, and seeking out the best bubble tea that the city has to offer. *@fiona_alice_* and *www.fionaalice.com*

Gina Fama Röckenwagner (she/her) is a colour-obsessed knitwear designer and artist based in Los Angeles, California. *@ginarockenwagner @soft_haus* and *www.softha.us*

Kiyomi + Sachiko Burgin (she/her) are twin sisters from Ontario, Canada. They live in different cities, but still talk daily, and knit together through video chat. They published their first knitting book, *Moon and Turtle* with Pom Pom Publishing. *@kiyomibee* and *@sachikobee*

Laura Chau (she/her) is a knitting designer and technical editor living in Toronto. She likes to design interesting-to-knit, wearable pieces for a variety of skill levels and styles. *@laurachau.designs and* Ravelry *@laurachau*

Rachel Coopey (she/her) is a knitwear designer with a focus on small, intricate, and wearable pieces. Socks are her favourite, and she brings her love of texture, pattern, and colour into every pair. See her latest designs in *Ready Set Socks*, published by Pom Pom Press. *@coopknits and coopknits.co.uk*

Sophie Heathscott (she/her) learned to knit when she was knee-high to a sheep, and after studying Design at Goldsmiths, London, she fully wove herself into the knitting world. She is passionate about how making creates community and provides a remedy for overconsumption. When not crafting you'll mostly find her baking, gardening, or punning.

Toshiyuki Shimada (he/him) was born in Japan. After studying music in Japan he went on to study around Europe, where he was inspired by many local knitters. He has practised handcrafts and painting since childhood, and eventually focused on knitting. He now teaches workshops across Europe and in Japan, and has published several knitting books. Find examples of his work at *#toshiyukishimada* and *#嶋田俊之*.

Abbreviations + Techniques

beg	Beginning
cast off	Bind off
ch	Chain (crochet)
dc	Double crochet (UK: treble crochet)
dec	Decrease
DPN(s)	Double-pointed needle(s)
foll	Follow(s)/Following
G st	Garter stitch
inc	Increase
k	Knit
k2tog	Knit 2 stitches together
k3tog	Knit 3 stitches together
kfb	Knit into the front and back of a stitch
kwise	Knitwise
LH	Left hand
M1	Work as M1L
M1L(P)	Make 1 Left; pick up strand between the two needles from the front to back with the tip of left needle, knit (purl) into the back of this stitch
M1R(P)	Make 1 Right; pick up strand between the two needles from back to front with the tip of left needle, knit (purl) into the front of this stitch
patt	Pattern (i.e. work in pattern)
PM	Place marker
p	Purl
p2tog	Purl 2 stitches together
pfb	Purl into the front and back of a stitch
PM	Place marker

pwise	Purlwise
rem	Remain(s)/Remaining
rep	Repeat
RH	Right hand
RS	Right side of fabric
s2kpo	Slip 2 stitches together knitwise, knit next stitch, pass slipped stitches over
sl	Slip
sl st	Slip stitch (crochet)
SM	Slip marker
sp	Space
ssk	Slip 2 stitches knitwise one at a time, knit together through the back loops
sssk	Slip 3 stitches knitwise one at a time, knit together through the back loops
st(s)	Stitch(es)
St st	Stocking stitch (stockinette): knit on RS rows, purl on WS rows
tbl	Through the back loop
tog	Together
wyib	With yarn held in back of work
wyif	With yarn held in front of work
WS	Wrong side of fabric
yo	Yarn over needle and into working position

Pom Pom tutorials for techniques used in this book are available at *pompommag.com/tutorials*

Backwards-Loop Cast-On   German Short Rows

Grafting   I-Cord

Long-Tail Cast-On

Yarn Support

Here's a handy list of the yarns we used in this book and where to get them. Can't find one of these yarns near you? Have a look at our substitutions advice on page 12 for help on choosing an alternative.

BC Garn
Summer in Kashmir GOTS
bcgarn.dk

Berroco
Ultra Wool DK
Berroco.com

Hedgehog Fibres
Sock Minis
shop.hedgehogfibres.com

John Arbon Textiles
Knit by Numbers DK
jarbon.com

Kelbourne Woolens
Germantown
kelbournewoolens.com

Malabrigo
Rios
Malabrigoyarn.com

Manos del Uruguay
Alegria
manos.uy

Neighborhood Fiber Co.
Studio DK
neighborhoodfiberco.com

Purl Soho
Home Life
purlsoho.com

Rauma Garn
Finull
raumagarn.no

Retrosaria Rosa Pomar
Mondim
retrosaria.rosapomar.com

Qing Fibre
Dashing DK
Qingfibre.com

The Uncommon Thread
BFL Light DK + Posh DK
theuncommonthread.co.uk

Mini Pom

Acknowledgements

Pom Pom can sometimes feel like a child we've reared and watched grow, and one that we've dressed in so very many pieces of knitwear along the way! It is such an honour to have reached a place where we can publish designs for kids based on our ten-year back catalogue.

We are so grateful to the knitwear designers featured in this book for trusting us with their patterns, many more than once, and for scaling them down to mini sizes. Pom Pom and this book would be nothing without their talents! As always, our Managing Editor, Amy Collins, turned this book from a years-long dream into a reality with the grace, patience, and enthusiasm that everyone loves her for. Sophie Heathscott was an indispensable piece of the *Mini Pom* puzzle, organising yarns, getting patterns tested, lending her expertise in the writing and tutorials, and, of course, contributing our mascot Truffle the pig to the design lineup. Alice Sleight lent her boundless expertise to grading our own designs into smaller sizes, in addition to Laura Chau and Chaitanya Muralidhara, both of whom also worked quickly and meticulously on the technical editing of this book. Our sample knitters were our saving grace - Chaitanya, Chonita, Rebecca, Kelly, and Sophie - we love you!

We are so thankful to Laura Morsman and her unique combination of talents - photography and a gentle way with kids. Annie Prime and Emi Ito took our writing and made it shine. Mary and Dan at Bless took all the parts and made them into a very adorable, readable, actual, real-life book!

The entire team at Pom Pom has been crucial to the production of *Mini Pom* - they pick up where we leave off, cheer us on, and make sure the finished product gets safely into your hands. So Belinda, Francesca, Gayle, Jasmine, and Noush, thank you for being a team we can so confidently depend on.

Meghan would like to thank the people who care for her own little kids while she's off writing and publishing books: their dad, their grandparents, and their wonderful teachers. And she's particularly grateful to her kids themselves, Sabine and Sylvie, for indulging her knitting whims, for being (mostly) willing fit models, and for giving their frank (and often unsolicited) opinions on kid knitwear.

Meghan + Lydia, Editors